A TECHNICAL MANUAL FOR CHURCH·PLANTERS

Duane Ruth-Heffelbower, JD, MDiv

Mennonite Board of Missions
Evangelism and
Church Development Department
Box 370 • Elkhart, Indiana 46515-0370

General Conference Mennonite Church
Commission on Home Ministries
Box 347 • Newton, Kansas 67114-0347

Published by Mennonite Board of Missions, Evangelism and Church Development Department, Box 370, Elkhart, Indiana 46515-0370
and
General Conference Mennonite Church, Commission on Home Ministries, Box 347, Newton, Kansas 67114-0347.
Design: Joy Frailey

ISBN 1-877736-01-5

Printed in the United States of America

Table of Contents

About the Author

Duane Ruth-Heffelbower is a California lawyer who, after 11 years of general practice, closed his law office to enter seminary studies in preparation for pastoral ministry. His practice included a variety of work with religious and secular nonprofit corporations, as well as various business and real estate matters. His personal business experience includes commercial real estate development, office building management, and service business management. He attended Mennonite Brethren Biblical Seminary in Fresno, California, and graduated from Associated Mennonite Biblical Seminaries, Elkhart, Indiana, receiving an MDiv in church planting/evangelism and pastoral counseling. Duane holds a BA in English from Kansas State University, and JD from Golden Gate University School of Law, San Francisco, California. He and his wife Clare Ann, a graduate of Mennonite Brethren Biblical Seminary, are co-pastors of a church planting project in Fresno, California, sponsored by the Pacific District Conference of the General Conference Mennonite Church (GCMC). Duane served nine years with the Division of Administration of GCMC, including service on the Development Committee and three years on the General Board. Duane is currently a member of the GCMC Spiritual Emphasis Committee. He has worked closely with Pacific District Conference on various matters and has served on inter-Mennonite and ecumenical groups. In addition to his pastoral duties, he practices professionally as a mediator. Duane's publications include *The Christian and Jury Duty* and *After We're Gone: Estate and Life Planning for a Disabled Person's Family*, both available through Mennonite Central Committee, Akron, Pennsylvania.

Preface

Frequently, leaders in church planting settings ask for organizational help. They want specific information about legal, tax, insurance, banking, finance and real estate areas. They need this information to create credibility with federal and state/provincial governments and the general populace around them.

Duane Ruth-Heffelbower was commissioned by the Evangelism and Church Development Departments of the General Conference Mennonite Church and the Mennonite Church to write this book as a companion model to the book, *Church Planting: From Seed to Harvest*, by Dale L. Stoll. Stoll's book deals with practical planning helps for use by conferences and denominations involved in planting new churches, and also serves these new congregations as a continuing guide for long-range planning and evaluation.

Duane Ruth-Heffelbower was asked to provide in this book technical, rather than program or theological, information for young congregations being developed. It is written with the perspective that these developing congregations will be independent in life and mission, but also related to a denominational body which can provide credentials for ministers, outside perspective, resources for mission and ministry, and a peer relationship which connects the congregation to the larger church body and world mission. This book will have primary significance for the Mennonite/Anabaptist bodies in North America, but it can easily be used by congregations affiliated with other Christian denominations.

This book aims to fill a gap not previously addressed in church planting/church development literature. We trust this information will help "prepare God's people for works of service, so that the body of Christ may be built up" (Ephesians 4:12 NIV).

- Irvin D. Weaver
  Mennonite Board of Missions
  Elkhart, Indiana

- Donald E. Yoder
  Commission on Home Ministries
  Newton, Kansas

- Rudy A. Regehr
  Congregational Resources Board
  Conference of Mennonites in Canada
  Winnipeg, Manitoba

Author's Preface

It is my belief that every decision a church planter makes needs to be submitted to God in prayer, and that every action should be done in attentiveness to God's direction. The procedures and suggestions offered here presume that attitude.

When leaders of a church show that their first concern is to wait upon and seek God's direction, the church will be well grounded. This book aims to describe processes compatible with that Spirit-led leadership. May all your efforts be blessed as you do your part to make God's reign visible in new churches.

—Duane Ruth-Heffelbower, Elkhart, Indiana, March 1988

I—LEADERSHIP and AFFILIATION
of a Church Planting Project

Churches plant churches,
and denominational groups plant churches.
Sometimes individuals plant churches.

This book speaks most directly to church planting done by members of a denomination which has regional conferences and congregational polity, although most of it also applies to independent church planters.

This book has some specific information regarding Mennonite organizational structures and ways of handling church planting projects. These examples apply to any denominational group which has a congregational polity. For groups with an episcopal polity, the flowcharts and other process information may be less useful. To use the flowcharts, simply write in the name of the parallel organization for your denomination.

We will discuss the preparation of a church planting proposal in Chapter II. Your situation determines to whom the proposal is made. What follows are two flowcharts. The one on the left (p. 2) is a hypothetical project originally discerned by a regional conference. The one on the right (p. 3) is a flowchart for the proposal made by my wife and me for planting a church in Fresno, California, under the sponsorship of Pacific District Conference of the General Conference Mennonite Church and in consultation with two nearby congragations which are members of that conference. Using these as a guide, work out your own flowcharts in the margins.

The flowchart on the right, or situations where the church planter first feels a call, describes how the process of how discernment might go.

In situations where a congregation initiates the project idea, members will want to involve the regional conference, and the process of discernment will be a joint one. A congregational discernment process may also help individuals begin to see themselves as part of the core group, and may be where pastoral leadership is identified. In some circles it is most common for pastoral leadership to be called from the sponsoring congregation. The existence of potential pastoral leadership may cause people in a congregation to begin thinking about church planting.

See flow-charts on next two pages.

The flowchart will look slightly different in each case, and quite different in some cases. The proposal goes to the sponsor to assist that group in the funding decision. The sponsor can be a congregation, regional conference, or combination. It is best for a congregation to be involved in sponsoring the new work, even if all funding comes from the regional conference. The sponsor may be a congregation, but funding may come in part from the regional conference from funds provided by a denominational agency. The key in all cases is broad consultation among those affected by the plan, and among those able to help. There is a funding proposal form in the Appendix for Mennonite Church persons to include in their proposals.

FLOWCHARTS FOR PROPOSALS

Use this space for your own flowchart.

Flowchart for Church Planting Proposal
Originated by Conference/District

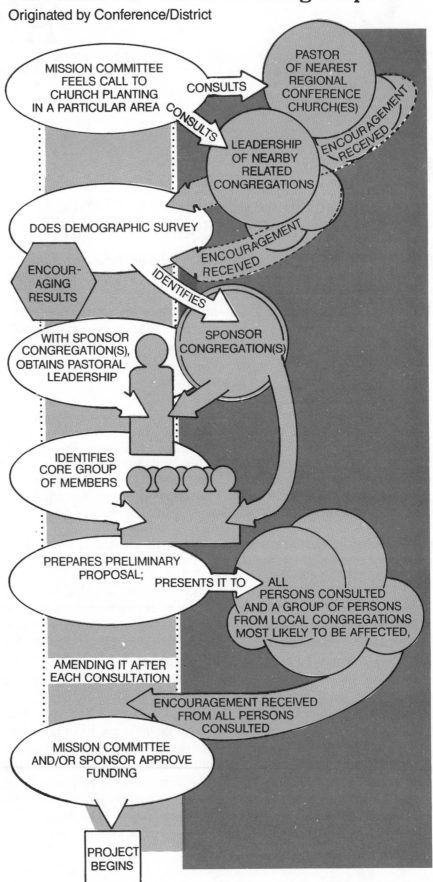

MISSION COMMITTEE FEELS CALL TO CHURCH PLANTING IN A PARTICULAR AREA

CONSULTS

CONSULTS

PASTOR OF NEAREST REGIONAL CONFERENCE CHURCH(ES)

ENCOURAGEMENT RECEIVED

LEADERSHIP OF NEARBY RELATED CONGREGATIONS

ENCOURAGEMENT RECEIVED

DOES DEMOGRAPHIC SURVEY

ENCOUR-AGING RESULTS

IDENTIFIES

SPONSOR CONGREGATION(S)

WITH SPONSOR CONGREGATION(S), OBTAINS PASTORAL LEADERSHIP

IDENTIFIES CORE GROUP OF MEMBERS

PREPARES PRELIMINARY PROPOSAL; PRESENTS IT TO

ALL PERSONS CONSULTED AND A GROUP OF PERSONS FROM LOCAL CONGREGATIONS MOST LIKELY TO BE AFFECTED,

AMENDING IT AFTER EACH CONSULTATION

ENCOURAGEMENT RECEIVED FROM ALL PERSONS CONSULTED

MISSION COMMITTEE AND/OR SPONSOR APPROVE FUNDING

PROJECT BEGINS

Flowchart for Church Planting Proposal

Originated by Church Planter/Individual

CALL TO CHURCH PLANTING

IN FRESNO AREA FELT

CONSULTS → MISSION COMMISSION TO SEE IF FRESNO IS A PRIORITY

CONSULTS → PASTOR OF EXISTING FRESNO CHURCH

ENCOURAGEMENT RECEIVED

REGIONAL CONFERENCE CHURCH PLANTING CONSULTANT

CONSULTS

CONSULTS → LEADERSHIP OF NEARBY CONGREGATION

ENCOURAGEMENT RECEIVED

ENCOURAGEMENT RECEIVED

ADVISED TO PREPARE PROPOSAL

DOES DEMOGRAPHIC SURVEY → ENCOURAGING RESULTS

PREPARES PRELIMINARY PROPOSAL, PRESENTING IT TO ALL

AND A GROUP OF PERSONS FROM LOCAL CONGREGATIONS MOST LIKELY TO BE AFFECTED

PERSONS CONSULTED

AMENDING IT AFTER EACH CONSULTATION

ENCOURAGEMENT RECEIVED FROM ALL PERSONS CONSULTED

PRESENTS PROPOSAL TO PACIFIC DISTRICT HOME MISSIONS COMMITTEE

PROPOSAL ACCEPTED FOR FUNDING; CALL AS CHURCH PLANTER CONFIRMED

Use this space for your own flowchart.

3. Leadership of a Church Planting Project

A. SUPERVISION

It is important for a church planter to be accountable to a person or group knowledgeable in church planting. Mennonite Church congregations are usually assigned an overseer, and a church planting project would share in that sort of supervision. General Conference Mennonite Church planting projects are usually related to the district church planting consultant.

B. SUPPORT GROUP

Support group becomes temporary board.

Each church planting project should have a support group which acts as its initial board. This support group would have one or two representatives of the regional conference (one of whom is from the locality of the church planting project), one or two from the sponsoring congregation, and one or two from the core group of the church planting project. It may be wise to include a local ecumenical member who is supportive of the project. That adds to the support group the viewpoint of a person knowledgeable about the area, but not personally involved in the project. The pastor of the new church would not be a member of the board, acting instead as the staff person who reports to the board. The pastor is responsible for leading, planning, implementing and organizing the programs of the emerging congregation. The pastor would be accountable to this support group; it would serve as the first board of directors of the new church when it incorporates (see Chapter III).

initial three-year term

The support group may not be complete for a while, since suitable core group members may not emerge for some time. Representatives of the regional conference and sponsoring congregation(s) need to be named as soon as possible after the project is accepted. Each member should agree to serve for three years, regardless of the length of their term on a regional conference or congregational board. This support group will be the sole board of the new church for the first two years, will be augmented by more members of the congregation at the second annual meeting, and will conclude their work at the third annual meeting. This will be explained in detail later.

As the new congregation begins to grow, it handles its own program decisions. The initial board exists to handle legal matters related to getting the church going, and as a group to whom the pastor can be accountable before the congregation can serve that purpose. In some situations, the transition from the initial board to a board of elected church members may be faster than in others. The suggestion in Chapter III is that two additional members be elected from the congregation in the second year, and all initial members be replaced in the third year.

In the initial stages of a church planting project, the pastor will need personal support and supervision. Some have found that support and supervisory functions need to be handled by different people. The pastor will be the principal carrier of the vision for the new congregation, but the support group must enthusiastically share that vision. It is important that members not be placed on the support group to "fill a slot," but rather for their excitement about the project and their ability to see the big picture. The support group, along with the pastor, will be responsible for reporting to the regional conference and sponsoring congregation(s). (Ongoing reporting forms can be found in Appendix F.)

C. PASTOR

Whether called a church planter (short-term) or a founding pastor (long-term), it is the pastor who is in charge of a church planting project. The pastor is responsible to the support group, but the support group is not the church planter. Churches are not planted by committee. Persons who first join the new congregation will do so, at least in part, because they want the church planter to be their pastor. This is different from an existing church where the program might go on without any input from the pastor, and where many people make a new person welcome. As the fledgling church grows, the person of the pastor becomes somewhat less important and the nature of the fellowship more important. You may have noted in the flowcharts above that the pastor was called before the core group was identified. It is important that the core group not just be in love with the idea of church planting. They must also be able to work with the particular pastor who will lead the group.

The pastor is in charge.

Where a core group identifies itself first and then begins a church planting project, careful work needs to be done with the pastor they hire to achieve a unified vision for the project. Failure to do this can tie up the project. The pastor should be part of the original visioning process, entering the discussion at the earliest possible phase. A group should avoid developing too specific a plan of ministry before the pastor is part of the group.

As time goes on, others will share this vision and begin to participate in shaping it. Those who began the project will need to gently release control as this begins to happen, guiding and encouraging without trying to control the growth and development of the vision. This process is critical to the health of the new church. Strength comes from the process of shaping competing visions of the church into one vision.

releasing control: pastor and core group

Personality type is an important consideration in a person's choice to become a church planter, and in a sponsor's decision to call a church planting pastor. While it is possible for an individual with any personality type to be a successful church planter, research and experience have indicated that certain personality types are better suited for church planting.

Church planting projects need very assertive pastors. Assertiveness is the willingness to take initiative in a way which empowers other members of the congregation rather than making them dependent. This may cause discomfort for a sponsoring congregation. Quite often the sponsor would not be comfortable with a pastor like the church planter it is sponsoring. That is as it should be. Both can learn from each other. It is important for the sponsoring congregation to recognize the different pastoral styles required for an existing church and a church planting project, so there will not be undue tension or any attempt to change the church planter into a less assertive leader too soon.

Assertive-ness is essential.

D. LICENSING/ORDINATION FOR PASTORAL LEADERSHIP

Some denominations ordain seminary graduates as a matter of course. It is customary among Mennonites to license new pastors immediately upon beginning pastoral duties in a congregation or church planting project. This designates them as approved ministers and acts as their credentials when dealing with government agencies. The sponsoring congregation would usually request licensure of a church planter by the regional conference through its ministerial committee.

A sample contract for the pastor can be found in Appendix C.

PASTOR: ORDINATION AND LICENSING

Mennonite groups look at ordination for a pastor who has been serving at least one or two years, as a recognition of a lifetime call to ministry.

From a practical perspective, most states and provinces require licensing or ordination of pastors before they can perform marriages, and the federal government requires it for self-employed tax status. It is sometimes necessary to show ministerial credentials when visiting persons in jails and hospitals. Mennonite practice is not uniform regarding which functions are reserved for the licensed or ordained, with the exception that only an ordained person can ordain another.

1. Different Models of Church Planting

In *Church Planting: From Seed to Harvest* by Dale Stoll, five models for a new church are described.

A **"congregational swarm"** describes a fairly large group leaving one congregation to start another. A **"cooperative swarm"** forms the new group from more than one supporting congregation. **"Congregational church planters"** are sent out by a congregation which has discerned their gifts for church planting and wants to support them in that venture. **"Relocated Mennonites"** (or members of any denomination) sometimes seek to start a church in an area distant from their home congregation. **"District or provincial church planters"** are selected, supported and sent to new areas by a regional conference for purposes of starting a new church from scratch.

To these forms we add a variation—**"cooperative church planters"**—people sponsored by a regional conference who are working in cooperation with one or more local congregations which shared in the decision to begin the work. A core group for the new congregation is built from the cooperating congregations and others. This makes a support group a necessary part of the plan, since the core group of the new church will need the perspective of others and of its sponsors. The support group provides a consulting forum for the various interested groups and a board for accountability on the pastor's part. Since no congregation will be officially formed for some time, having a legal entity in place is important.

cooperative church planters

The six models break into two types—those which have a congregation in the beginning, and those which do not. The initial organization of the project is quite different for these two types. A swarm and a fellowship of relocated people are both cases where there is a group ready to be a new church, but which needs pastoral leadership and often financial support. Regional conference and cooperative church planters are completely dependent on the sponsor for financial support and organizational assistance as they begin to form a new group with no previous identity. As we look at the steps for beginning, keep these two types in mind.

Pastors who provide a portion of their own support by working outside the church are called **"tentmakers"** after the Apostle Paul. Any of the models can have a tentmaker as pastor.

"tentmaking"

2. Preparing a Proposal for a Church Planting Project

A. STEPS IN PREPARING TO WRITE THE PROPOSAL

examining motives for a new church

Swarms begin in different ways. The final result is a group of people within a congregation or group of congregations who feel called to begin a new church. Their task then becomes one of obtaining support from the parent congregation(s), sometimes including financial support. When this support is given, the parent congregation(s) then become the "sponsor" of the project. To obtain this support, the swarm group will need to prepare a proposal describing their project, and describe the kind of assistance they want. It is important that the process leading to the proposal be open, inviting consultation from anyone interested. It is too easy for a swarm to become a split by inadequate processing before the actual proposal is presented. Is the motivation of the group stemming from excitement about carrying out the Great Commission, or is it motivated by dissatisfaction? Congregations have difficulty supporting groups which are leaving because of unhappiness.

Regional conference church planters are in a different situation since they begin with a sponsor already convinced about the project. How can the regional conference convey its hopes and dreams for the project to the church planter in a way which will adequately communicate? One suggestion is that the church planter, in consultation with the appropriate persons from the sponsor, prepare a proposal for the project as described below. This will give ample opportunity to negotiate and will avoid much misunderstanding. It will also permit building an adequate budget. It is better if the church planter has been involved with the development of the project from the beginning, but that is unusual in this model.

Relocated persons who believe they want to undertake a church planting project need to think carefully before writing a proposal. What is the motivation? Do they want a fellowship group of persons of similar background, or do they want a church? A church, by definition, is involved in calling persons to new life in Christ and nurturing that new life. Is that your call? The process of writing a proposal may be very helpful in discerning the group's call to church planting.

Cooperative church planters are somewhat more likely to have been involved in the process from the beginning due to the involvement of congregations in the decision. When a congregation is involved in discerning the need for a new local church planting project, it is more likely to have leadership in mind than a conference would be, and it is also likely that the discernment process will identify leadership. After considerable discussion, the church planter prepares a proposal as is being discussed here, and that proposal is amended after further consultation. The final proposal is adopted by the regional conference, which acts as the funding sponsor.

The preparation for writing a proposal is important, since it is the process by which a sponsor begins to see itself in that role, and the church planter is able to test the specific call. We often talk of a call to ministry for the pastor, but the sponsoring congregation's call to ministry is just as important in church planting. The process of preparation is one of mutual discernment.

B. WHAT TO INCLUDE

If you are using **Church Planting: From Seed to Harvest,** this section corresponds to "The Preliminary Plan" on page 17. Coming to this point presumes that a feasibility study has been done and the sponsoring group, swarm or church planter has decided to prepare a proposal for presentation to potential sponsoring congregations and/or a regional conference mission committee. This presumes that any decision to plant a church is a mutual one between a regional conference and either an existing local congregation (where there is one) or a church planter. The regional conference's congregation nearest the project should be involved in the decision, whether they are being asked to serve as sponsor or not. Where there are cooperating regional conferences in an area, the decision of one to proceed with a church planting project should be processed with the others. What follows is an annotated version of Dale Stoll's suggested contents for a proposal.

Include a preliminary mission statement, philosophy of ministry, list of goals and an action plan in the proposal. They are preliminary because they are still a part of the feasibility study. When the proposal is adopted and work begins, these preliminary matters become working statements.

The mission statement gives the project's initial direction, and it enables people to distinguish this church from another. As the work begins, there may be many shifts in direction. As that happens, the mission statement should be kept up to date. The **mission statement** should include:

1. The reasons this church is being planted
2. The type of church being planted
3. The area and groups targeted
4. The primary and secondary sponsors
5. The denominational and regional conference affiliations expected

Preparing a **philosophy of ministry** before pastoral leadership is identified can be a problem, since the task then becomes one of finding a leader who agrees with a philosophy on paper. When an established congregation calls a pastor, the pastor can see what the congregation is doing. In a new church planting situation, pastoral leadership should be involved in developing the philosophy of ministry since they will be the ones primarily charged with carrying the vision. The less fixed the philosophy of ministry is prior to obtaining pastoral leadership, the more likely the project will succeed. With that caution in mind, the philosophy of ministry should address the following questions:
1. What type of leadership will be sought? Will it be full-time, part-time or self-supporting? What will be expected of the leadership?
2. How will congregational oversight be provided? Who will walk with the leadership and the congregation as it evolves? What will be expected of the overseer?
3. What will make this church a Mennonite church (or other denomination)?
4. What worship style will predominate?
5. What will be the strategy for evangelism?

Setting **goals** for the new church is both impossible and vital. What should the new church accomplish in its first year, two years, five years? These are the goals. The goals need to be specific, achievable and measurable. If there is no way to tell whether a goal has been met, it is not a proper goal. It is advisable to set firm goals for the first year, and tentative annual goals for five years. They can be updated each year, adding a new fifth year. It is usual to plan more than can be done in one year, and much less than can be done in five years, so think bigger. In the first year's planning, include specific objectives to be met within the year, which will lead you toward the goal.

Refer to: Church Planting: from Seed to Harvest.

See Appendix E for a proposal worksheet.

philosophy of ministry

Specify roles to avoid hurt feelings.

CHURCH PLANTING PROPOSAL

Set growth and budget goals.

It is important to set growth goals and budget goals. Specific budget projections are necessary for the first several years, particularly if it involves a request for a grant from the sponsor. (Budgets are covered more fully in Chapter VI.) Mennonite Board of Missions, General Conference Mennonite Church, and Congregational Resources Board of the Conference of Mennonites in Canada have developed funding request forms. (Copies of these forms are in Appendix E.) Also found in Appendix E is Mennonite Board of Missions "Funding Principles for Partnership Grants with Conferences." Usually there are phase-out provisions by which subsidy is eliminated over a five-year period. General Conference Mennonite Church district and provincial conferences follow similar guidelines.

pastor's salary

One aspect of budget is the pastor's salary. Both the Mennonite Church and General Conference Mennonite Church (as well as other denominations) provide salary guidelines. Current copies are available to use in budget projections. Any deviations from it should be explained in the proposal. If a group cannot afford to pay a full salary, it is preferable to employ the pastor on a part-time basis rather than at a low salary for full-time service. It will be easier to increase the amount of paid time than to give a salary increase. If the church receives full-time work for part-time pay, it will be lulled into a false understanding of what it costs to be a church.

See Appendix E for funding request forms.

The process of creating a church planting proposal is an important aspect of the total project. Through this process, people involved begin to pull in the same direction. When the proposal is complete, it is presented to the appropriate group for approval.

C. SAMPLE: COMPLETE PROPOSAL

What follows is the proposal prepared by my wife Clare Ann and me after numerous consultations with sponsoring groups and faculty at the seminary where we were students. Every consultation resulted in changes to the proposal. It is presented here not as an ideal proposal, but as a real one. My comments on the proposal follow it.

Preliminary Mission Statement and Philosophy of Ministry
For a Mennonite church to be planted in Fresno, California

Why is this church to be planted?

- To respond to Jesus' commission given in Matthew 28:19-20 to make disciples of all people. It will specifically attempt to reach persons who are currently unchurched.
- To strengthen the Anabaptist/Mennonite witness in Fresno County.
- To strengthen the Anabaptist/Mennonite cluster of churches in Fresno County for purposes of mutual support and cooperation in various aspects of their ministries.
- To provide a different style Mennonite church than those currently available, creating an opportunity to reach people who are not part of existing congregations.

What kind of church is to be planted?

The intention is to plant a Mennonite church with what might be called an Anabaptist/evangelical flavor. It will have a solid foundation in Jesus Christ and will look to the Bible and the Holy Spirit for guidance. It will have the Anabaptist distinctives of discipleship, service, community and peacemaking. It will be assertive in sharing the good news of God's shalom with the larger community.

The areas in which this congregation will focus its energies are worship, witness and service to the community, and spiritual and personal growth and caring in its life together.

WORSHIP will be a priority. Worship will combine formal and informal elements in a warm, inviting style. A variety of musical styles will be used, with an overall upbeat and enthusiastic feel. Affective aspects of worship will be as important as cognitive aspects, and appeal to unchurched persons will be an initial priority.

SMALL GROUPS will be the basic unit of the congregation. All persons will be encouraged to be in groups. Caring within the congregation and ministries outside the congregation will occur largely through small groups. As people feel called to outreach ministries, groups would be formed to support those new ministries. Discipling new attenders will take place in small groups.

SIZE goal for worship attendance will be 300-400 people. This means the church will be multi-cell. It is hoped that continued strong growth would result in other churches being planted, and full use of leadership gifts within the congregation would be encouraged through such outward foci. It is hoped that rented space could be used until attendance reaches the 300-400 range so that a more realistic appraisal of worship space needs could be made at that point. No arbitrary size limits are envisioned at this time. From the beginning, the organization will be multi-cell to facilitate growth, and continued strong growth will be a goal from the beginning. Rather than creating a generic evangelical church which appeals to everyone, we intend to create a distinctively Anabaptist church which will gather those to whom it appeals.

Where is this church to be planted?

It is to be planted in Fresno, California. Location of the worship space is a variable which cannot yet be determined. The focus of our demographic work has been the southeast quadrant of the city of Fresno. Best worship space probabilities are on the west edge and north edge of this zone, which includes Fresno Pacific College, the Western Regional Internal Revenue Service headquarters, and opens to the south and east into the rural area toward Sanger and Reedley. This church would not be on the parish model, but would draw people from the entire metropolitan and surrounding rural areas on the basis of its distinctiveness. Worship space location convenient to freeways and main arterial streets will be a key consideration.

The southeast quadrant of Fresno has a complete mix of housing styles. It includes many new apartments and single-family dwellings. The primary direction of Fresno metropolitan growth has been to the north, and the southeast has been neglected by churches. Mennonite Community Church is on the north edge of the area we are discussing, and Butler Avenue Mennonite Brethren Church is within the area. A new Baptist church is the only growing evangelical church in the southeast quadrant of the city, and it has now built a building which will keep it small in size.

What group of persons will this church hope to attract?

It will focus on middle-class persons. While not setting out to be exclusive, we recognize the fact that church planters tend to attract people like themselves. The group with which we have had most affinity are "Yuppies," and that group would be a particular focus for us. Because the people with whom we have most natural affinity are in their child rearing years, strong children's programs will be an important factor. We are also experienced in dealing with adults at life stage transition points and various groups which are typically marginalized in the church, such as divorced persons and individuals living in nontraditional lifestyles. Reaching such persons will be a goal, although it will certainly not transcend the family orientation of the majority of the group.

Who will sponsor this church?

We are seeking funding primarily from the Pacific District Conference of the General Conference Mennonite Church. We anticipate a close working relationship with the local General Conference churches—Mennonite Community in Fresno and First Mennonite in Reedley. In the first two years, we hope this would include some financial support. We plan for the new church to be completely self-supporting within two years.

Both churches have had discussion of this proposal within their official structures, and those structures have affirmed it in general outline. A meeting of about 25 persons from those two churches and some Mennonite Brethren persons was held; that group affirmed the plan and encouraged us to pursue the project.

How will this church be planted?

We would begin with gathering a core of people who will meet regularly in small groups for six months or so prior to the first formal worship service. (As of this writing, ten people are identified as wanting to begin the core group. Additional persons have expressed interest.)

We also plan to use telemarketing. Twenty thousand people will be telephoned over a four- to six-week period, with a goal of having 200 of those persons attend the first formal worship service. Members of the core group and the supporting churches will do the telephoning, as well as other things which will be necessary prior to the first worship service. Part of the core building process will include discerning ministry gifts of core members and equipping those persons to use their gifts in the church. A core group of 40-50 persons prior to the first formal worship service is the goal.

When will this church be planted?

We moved back to Fresno in June 1988. We plan to officially start working on the church in September, with a goal of having the first formal worship service in the spring of 1989, perhaps Easter Sunday. The telephone campaign will begin Ash Wednesday.

What sort of pastoral leadership will this church have?

We will work together as co-pastors, filling one full-time position in the beginning. In church planting terminology, we see ourselves as founding pastors who have a long-term commitment to the new church rather than church planters who simply begin a church and move on. Final responsibility for different areas would be divided between us, even though we would both be involved in some areas, such as preaching, teaching and care giving. We see ourselves as part of a team ministry, with members of the congregation being important members of the team. Priority will be given to equipping members to be actively involved in the ministry team. We presume that as the church grows, additional staff persons would become part of the team, and that our time involvement would increase. We expect to use members of the core group and seminary interns to complete staffing in the beginning before giving and leadership from new attenders is a significant factor.

Strong pastoral leadership is vital to a venture such as this one, and we expect to give that sort of leadership. We are well aware that discipling 200 new people who arrive on the same day is a task beyond our strength, and trust that the Holy Spirit will work through the team that is gathered to accomplish the task and build the church.

Clare Ann and Duane Ruth-Heffelbower
September 29, 1987

Fresno Church Planting Project Budget Proposal

sample budget

This project presumes a first year beginning September 1, 1988. Staff would start core group formation at that time, and use the telemarketing plan during Lent 1989, resulting in a first worship service for 200 persons Easter Sunday, March 26, 1989. Duane and Clare Ann Ruth-Heffelbower will serve as co-pastors on one full-time equivalent basis. Office and worship space will be acquired no later than January 1, 1989, with office space September 1, 1988, preferred and budgeted. The second year's budget would have all of the above in place for the full year. Additional staff for youth and Christian education would be sought on an internship basis.

Budget Item	Fiscal 1988-89	Fiscal 1989-90 (note 5)
Pastoral Staff (note 1)		
Base		
Benefits		
Subtotal		
Telemarketing, including		
Phone and Printing (note 2)		
Rent (note 3)		
Rent for Worship Equipment		
Office Supplies		
Start-up Expenses		
Signs, Small Equipment		
Staff Conference Travel		
Automobile Expense		
Service on Equipment		
Subtotal		
Expenditure		
Grand Total		

Actual figures were deleted from this budget to avoid dating the material and making specific dollar recommendations that might not apply in another geographical or organizational situations.

capital expenses

Notes

Capital items not included in the budget are office equipment and sound equipment (note 4). The proposal is for Pacific District Conference (PDC) to loan the new church $7,000 on an as-needed basis for the purchase of these items, with payback to be over a five-year period beginning the third fiscal year. There would be no interest, and contributions from the church for PDC budget would be applied to the loan, so that more rapid amortization is likely. This plan allows for flexibility in the acquisition of capital items, and part of the agreement would be for the items to revert to PDC in the event the new church dissolved.

13

CHURCH PLANTING PROPOSAL • BUDGET

**Fresno Church Planting Project
Income Budget**

Pacific District (note 6)

Raised Locally

Duane and Clare Ann Ruth-Heffelbower
September 29, 1987

Total Income

Notes to Budget

1. Pastor's salary based on September 1, 1987, General Conference Mennonite Church guidelines, making a composite of Duane and Clare Ann, adding her experience and deleting his additional degree.

FYE 1989-90, add $300 to base for experience and three percent to base (except Social Security) for cost of living increase, recalculating other items as needed.

Base Fiscal 1988-89 Fiscal 1989-90
Pastor w/multiple staff
Church size 101-300
Experience - three years
Small city
Social Security @ 6.51 percent
   Subtotal

Benefits
Medical - MMA
Retirement - 10 percent of base
Continuing education, books, etc.
   Subtotal

Total

2. Telemarketing. This budget item comes from an examination of the materials compiled by the Friends Church Southwest Yearly Meeting as adjusted for our setting. It includes phone, printing, postage, mailing list creation (including purchase of street address directory information, etc.), and our attendance at the Southwest Yearly Meeting seminar on use of the method which includes a set of their materials. Twenty thousand phone calls would, according to well-established experience, generate a mailing list of 2,000 persons and result in 200 attending the first worship service. Servicing this mailing list would be a massive job requiring a computer. Mass mailings would be a continuing feature of this ministry.

3. Rent. This figure presumes an office from September 1, 1988, at $250 per month and worship space from January 1, 1990, at $400 per month. It would be preferable to begin paying for worship space March 1, 1990, but that seems unlikely. We have looked into space which would combine office and worship space for a lower total monthly outlay, but that would mean beginning the payments earlier. We have a year in which to check things out, and the market a year from this writing is difficult to forecast.

Worship equipment rental is mostly chairs. We may have a situation where chairs are provided, or a situation where it would be better to buy chairs. The two-year rental budget would cover purchase. There may or may not be a need to acquire a keyboard instrument (which would fit best under the capital equipment budget).

4. Office equipment includes a computer for word processing and mailing list maintenance, as well as literature preparation. An adequate system will run $1,500. This word processing equipment would also delay the day when paid secretarial help would be needed. Also included is $3,000 for a photocopier. It is possible, but not to be counted on, that we could obtain a used one for less. This would be a critical component due to a high volume of printing. Because we

14

have a good deal of office equipment, including an IBM typewriter, $500 should cover the additional furniture and set-up needs. A portable sound system will probably be needed, and we presume $2,000 capital expenditure for that.

Office supplies go up the second year as the telemarketing supplies run out.

5. Not budgeted, but presumed for the second year, is an increase in pastor's time and some paid staff, such as secretarial. This would depend on giving. We would anticipate sufficient giving by new attenders to do these things, add equipment, and begin supporting General Conference Mennonite Church and Pacific District Conference (PDC) through special offerings. It would also be necessary to begin building a bank balance to offset the subsidy when it ended.

6. Total request from PDC for the two-year period is $38,749.02, after which we anticipate being self-supporting. This is an average of $7,749.80 over a five-year period, the norm for traditional church planting projects.

end of proposal

Comments on the Proposal

Some things have changed as I update this in October 1988. We are in the midst of the telephone campaign, and are planning a January 8 first worship service. This is a substantial change in timing. We had no media or advertising budget, but the telephoning will be much cheaper thanks to donated telephones and space. This will allow the telemarketing budget to cover more. We were also pleased to be able to rent a school building, which means our rent will be as budgeted and will not start several months before worship services. All of these savings are important since the core group has changed into a small task group rather than a larger nurture group, and so cannot contribute significantly to the budget.

One particularly helpful financial device has been to capitalize the telemarketing budget item, and to use conference loan funds to cover it rather than having those expenses come from our regular budget. Meeting for worship in a school means that we have not had the equipment expenses originally planned, and that made loan funds available which had earlier been targeted for equipment.

3. Denominational Affiliation

A. WHY AFFILIATE WITH A REGIONAL CONFERENCE?

Many church planters are on their own these days. The model of a tentmaker pastor knocking on doors to gather people for a Bible study group is alive and well. For Mennonites, our history of congregational autonomy lends itself to asking the question, "Why join a conference?" Our regional conferences have not paid church planters large salaries year after year, so what is gained by giving up any autonomy by joining, particularly when the regional conference has no actual power over the congregation?

Mennonites take **mutual submission** very seriously. This means that within a congregation there is at least some accountability for one another, and some duty to exercise discipline when a person strays. Between congregations it means the same thing, with assistance of various kinds being given to those in need. Loans and grants are available for congregtaions from various church agencies. Mennonites have formed health and fire insurance agencies, making much of their sharing less direct than it once was. Even so, these agencies exist for members of Mennonite congregations only.

mutual submission and accountability

15

In regional conference sessions, issues of faith and practice are worked through, looking for consensus on matters difficult to understand. There is a sharing of costs in the publication of educational materials, operation of educational institutions, and sending of mission workers. Members of the regional conference benefit from these ministries and help to shape them. Regional conferences can form a united voice for speaking out on a variety of issues. Only members can shape that voice.

A congregation can do without any of these things. A congregation that is not connected with other congregations through a regional conference is similar to an individual who is not connected with other Christians in a church. Without that connection, the separated one is the loser. The volatility of a new congregation needs to be tempered and mellowed by relationship to a group of congregations which are not volatile. The more staid congregations benefit from the new ones as well, just as individual Christians benefit from being with excited new Christians. The price of regional conference membership, it seems to me, is low compared to the benefits.

B. WHEN SHOULD A
NEW CONGREGATION AFFILIATE?

As stated above, the decision to begin a new church should be made by the sponsor, the church planter and the regional conference to which they relate. To begin a new work without consulting the regional conference can be very wasteful. The regional conference is a resource for finding what has already been explored, what help is available, and who is already working on similar projects.

Denominational membership is handled differently depending on the denomination. The General Conference Mennonite Church meets every three years; it is at those times that new congregations can join. Membership in a district or provincial conference does not make a congregation a member of the General Conference Mennonite Church.

This is just the reverse with the Mennonite Church. Joining a conference makes a congregation a member of the Mennonite Church General Assembly. There is little practical difference in daily practice. Both denominations prefer to work through regional conferences, but will service a congregation directly where appropriate.

C. HOW DOES A CONGREGATION
AFFILIATE WITH A CONFERENCE?

Contacting the regional conference officers or regional conference minister is the best way to get started. Each group has a process for admitting a new group. Church planting projects of a regional conference are admitted as a matter of course during the annual meeting. Involving the regional conference early in your planning will make the project go much more easily.

III–ORGANIZING for ACTION

The decision has been made to proceed with a church planting project. Leadership is in place. Funding has been approved by the sponsor. This chapter describes the process of becoming a legal entity, and of dealing with tax, banking and accounting issues. Traditionally church planters have been slow to deal with these issues due to lack of understanding, or because they believe the congregation must determine its stance on doctrinal issues before it can take on structural issues.

You will want to develop a **statement of faith** for the new congregation separate from your legal documents. Your denominational statement can be used as a starting point. The legal details can be handled by the support group or core group before a congregation is formed, so that the congregation can focus on its life together.

statement of faith

The process of developing a constitution takes energy which could otherwise be spent on program. This time is often wasted in a new church since the constitution will need regular adjustments as experience is gained. It is also common for a church to embed in its constitution all sorts of changeable details. The model constitution/bylaws provided here cover only the necessary details of legal existence, leaving it to the church's program boards to develop policies and procedures for running the program of the church. Any of the details of this model can be changed. Check with your attorney to make sure you have complied with the legal minimum requirements.

1. Creating a Legal Entity

A. INCORPORATION VERSUS UNINCORPORATED ASSOCIATION

A **legal entity** is created whenever a group of people agree to do something together. Whether that legal entity is a joint venture, association, partnership, corporation or some combination is the question. A church can be an **unincorporated association,** or a **corporation** in most jurisdictions (state, province, country). Virginia and West Virginia, for instance, do not allow churches to incorporate. Each jurisdiction has statutes (written laws created by the legislature) which describe the nature of a church from a legal standpoint. It is important for church planters to know what laws apply to a church in their jurisdiction; a lawyer is the person to consult on those questions.

creating a legal entity

Generally speaking, being incorporated is the best course for a church (where permitted). Most jurisdictions protect the members of a nonprofit corporation from being liable for the debts of the corporation, but hold members of unincorporated associations liable for the debts of the association. While no one suggests that church members walk away from the debts of the church,

Incorporation is preferred.

few believe that individual members of the church ought to be personally liable for its debts. These debts could include large amounts for injuries to persons at church events or other things which church members may have little control over. Find out what the law is in your jurisdiction. It is presumed here that your church will want to incorporate. The section on formation documents applies equally well to churches which will not be incorporated.

B. PROFESSIONAL CONSULTANTS TO OBTAIN

Lawyer

obtaining a lawyer

When forming a legal entity, it is important to consult with a lawyer familiar with the type of organization being formed. Not every lawyer is equipped to consult with a church planter. A lawyer active and interested in the church may be more help than an experienced but disinterested one, if the job is done. Check with other churches for names of lawyers experienced in church work.

Choose wording carefully.

An interested lawyer can help handle structure issues. It is important not to be creative with the legal structure of your church without a creative lawyer being part of the process. Many horror stories exist where churches made simple changes to their bylaws which accidentally eliminated other items of major importance. One church wanted to use a discernment process rather than voting to decide whether to retain pastors, so they wrote the discernment process into their constitution and dropped the voting sections. As the next set of officers began to work with a less than adequate pastor, they discovered that the church literally had no way to terminate a pastor. They were stuck with hoping for a timely resignation. Consider what sorts of things a dissatisfied congregation can do to help the pastor's decision making along. It is better to have clear lines of authority and accountability.

Accountant

Get a professional with experience.

Almost anyone can successfully keep books of account, but setting up those accounts in the first place is not an amateur's job. Borrowing the accounting procedures of an existing church is a good way to inherit problems. Go to an accountant (CPA, chartered or some similar designation) and discuss the situation. Ask the accountant(s) whether he or she has any churches as clients, or experience in setting up church accounting systems.

Let the accountant educate your treasurer.

You will have the normal incomes and expenses of any business, but will also have trust accounts for various forms of charitable giving. Have the accountant set up your books and show your treasurer how to work with them. When you change treasurers, send the new one to the accountant to learn the system, as well as having the former treasurer assist in the transition. If the new treasurer is not trained, the mistakes and shortcuts taken by the last treasurer will be compounded. Make it a known policy that the **new treasurer will always consult with the accountant,** not just when the last treasurer was inadequate. That will eliminate hurt feelings.

eliminating temptation

It is important to note here that embezzlement happens in churches as in any other business. It is easier to steal from a church because the bookkeeping is done by volunteers who trust each other. Do not tempt people to steal by having loose procedures for handling money, particularly cash. When offerings are taken, the money should be in the presence of two people until the deposit slip is made. The full amount received should be deposited. Deposits should always be checked against the permanent deposit slip copies. All spending should be by check, and someone besides the person writing the checks should compare the canceled checks against the check record. If you care about your people, you will set up systems which eliminate both temptation and any possible appearance of wrongdoing which might result in suspicion or false accusation. An accountant can help you do this.

As a church grows, particularly as it becomes involved in a building project, a volunteer treasurer will begin having more work than was agreed upon. Your financial statements are likely to get shorter, slower, and generally less helpful. Consider having your accountant handle the book-keeping and reporting functions. Most will have computer systems which allow your treasurer to give a list of income and disbursements, and to receive complete reports quickly, in helpful form. This need not be expensive. Check into it. Cheap accounting can become expensive if you lose track of the church's performance.

Pay by checks only.

Other Consultants

In the beginning, you may use a marketing consultant to help identify target areas and devise growth strategies, a direct mail consultant if you are using that method, graphic artists to prepare literature, real estate people, church planting consultants, insurance advisers and others. Some of this advice is free, and some is not.

Care and Nurture of Professional Consultants

Professional consultants earn their living consulting. All they have to sell is their time and advice. You will not be the first or last worthy cause to come to them. Even if they are members of your denomination or core group, presume nothing. Ask at the first meeting, before any advice is given, what their fee structure is. Plan to pay for their services. It is true that many professionals will give free or discounted services to churches, especially of their own denomination, but do not presume that. Many professionals prefer to be paid, then donate an equivalent amount back. It is important to many professionals that their clients behave like clients. That includes being prompt with payment and needed information. If you do not behave like a client, it may be difficult for the professional to treat you like one.

Plan to pay for services.

A caution about free service is in order. If you are not paying for a service, you will receive it when it is convenient to the professional. Free services do not pay the overhead.

Churches should behave like clients when using professional consultants. This includes making it clear who speaks for the church. Preferably, two people should go together for appointments with professionals. That reduces misunderstandings of the advice given. For a church planting project, it makes sense for the church planter or founding pastor to be one of those people. Larger groups may breed confusion and dilute the value of the time spent with the consultant, as more explaining needs to be done to bring everyone to the same level of understanding.

C. HOW TO INCORPORATE

Articles of Incorporation

The simple answer is: File Articles of Incorporation with the Secretary of State, Provincial Officer or equivalent of your jurisdiction.

In the Appendix you will find sample Articles of Incorporation. In the U.S., write to the Secretary of State (or equivalent) in your state capital for information regarding incorporation of a church. A letter addressed "Provincial Officer, Corporation Division, Capital City, Province," will do the job in Canada. As indicated in the Appendix, some states and provinces have a printed form of articles. In other jurisdictions they must be typed. The only decisions you need to make, in most cases, are your corporate name, and the number and names of your incorporators. Do not use the forms in the Appendix since those change annually. Have your lawyer provide you with the proper form, and discuss with you the implications of the choices available.

where to write

ARTICLES OF INCORPORATION • BYLAWS

irrevocable dedication clause

One technicality in U.S. Articles of Incorporation is the **irrevocable dedication clause.** This paragraph must be included for federal tax exemption purposes. It is in technical language, but basically says that the property of the corporation is irrevocably (forever) dedicated to charitable purposes, and that none of it will ever be given to private individuals for their own use in the event the corporation dissolves. In most jurisdictions you can specify your regional conference as the recipient of the assets of your church if the church dissolves.

choosing a name

Church planting projects often bog down at this stage of the organizational process, being unable to choose a name, or not knowing how to go about choosing a name. The name should be chosen very early in the process when there are fewer people to please; consult your support group and don't think the name is permanent. It is rare for a church to be known by the first name it chooses. Try to avoid geographically specific names which won't survive a move to new worship space. For the new church to grow, you need to attract new people. Choose a name which sounds attractive to your target group; don't be afraid to change it when that would be best. Each jurisdiction has rules about names, and only one group may have a name in each jurisdiction. Check those rules with your attorney.

chartering service

Who will the incorporators be? Some churches have had a **formal chartering service** where all of the founding members sign the Articles of Incorporation. That is nice in its own way, but what was going on during the time prior to that service? One suggestion is for the church to be incorporated immediately when the project begins, using members of the support group as incorporators. This group of around five people will include regional conference officers or staff, a member or two of the sponsoring group, and a member or two of the initial core group, where there is one. Since this is the board to whom the pastor is accountable, the pastor should not be a member of the group of incorporators. This group will form the legal ownership of the corporation until that role is turned over to a board named by the congregation two or three years later.

Why this procedure? For one thing, it makes the new church "real" at the very beginning. It gives the pastor a legal board to consult and be accountable to. It protects the pastor by making decisions which affect the pastor's salary and benefits. It provides a solid link to the sponsor group. It assures a structure for handling money and property. It creates a legal entity capable of signing leases and buying equipment in its own name. It protects the members from individual liability for the church's debts. It ensures that the project will continue in the direction it began by preventing a few new members from turning the property of the new church to other uses. It allows a church structure to be adopted by someone other than the pastor for use until the new church becomes self-governing. It protects the pastor from sudden shifts within the rapidly growing and changing congregation. It keeps the new church oriented toward its sponsoring body and regional conference, and ensures consultation with those groups before major new thrusts are undertaken. An important benefit from this procedure is that the new church can focus on group building instead of arguing about structure.

Bylaws/Constitution

The bylaws, also sometimes known as a constitution, presume incorporation by a small group and provide transitional provisions. A group which waits to incorporate until it is large enough and stable enough to be self-governing would leave out the transitional provisions, as might a church planted by the "swarm" method from a parent congregation.

Bylaws are to be adopted by the incorporators after the Articles of Incorporation are filed with the Provincial Officer or Secretary of State.

Model Bylaws/Constitution

At the beginning of Chapter II we discussed six models of church planting. These models have more in common than not. The bylaws below apply to these models, and are to guide you in your discussions with a lawyer. Each state or province has peculiarities which need to be taken into account in writing bylaws. Of particular importance in these forms are the paragraphs relating to the formation of the initial board from the support group and transition to congregational self-government. These paragraphs are not "stock" forms which lawyers will have. They exist only here. Much of the material in this set of model bylaws is found in standard lawyers' reference works. Giving this book to your lawyer will make discussion of the plan easier.

The presuppositions at work in these forms are that the church planting project has been fully approved by whoever needs to approve it; that pastoral leadership is in place ("the pastor" is used to include co-pastors); that there is a sponsoring body; that the project relates to a regional conference body on at least an area basis, if not a national basis; that a support group is formed as outlined above; and that there is a desire to follow through on legal formalities in a businesslike way.

These model bylaws may seem foreign to you. They do not sound like a church document. They seem to be preparing for things we don't foresee happening in the church. They suffer from legalese, although I have worked at cleaning up the language. The rationale for various provisions is given in notes within the body of the bylaws or at the end. [Brackets] indicate something not to be included in a final draft of the bylaws, either because it is a note or because it marks a blank to be filled in. (Parentheses) set out parenthetical matter to be retained in the bylaws. You may find it most helpful to read the section on organizational presuppositions following the bylaws before reading the bylaws themselves.

Most things in these bylaws could be changed without creating a problem. Where your situation requires a change, remember there are probably other sections which are affected, and an ambiguity can easily be created if you do not locate all the places where a change is needed. Notice requirements are a good example of technical items which must be coordinated throughout. It is better to make only those changes which are necessary for your situation. Be sure to have your final result reviewed by a lawyer, since lawyers are accustomed to looking for ambiguity and inconsistency in documents.

Remember that these bylaws do not have much affect on the day-to-day operation of the church. They only deal with issues of final, legal authority in the business dealings of the church.

MODEL BYLAWS/CONSTITUTION

[**WARNING:** These forms are intended for use only by attorneys duly admitted to the practice of law in the jurisdiction in which they are used. They are illustrative of the concepts contained in this book and are not intended as legal advice to any person or entity. No opinion is given by the author or publisher of the legal effect of any of the provisions of these bylaws in any particular jurisdiction. It is presumed by the author and publisher that these forms will require modification by a licensed attorney before use, since they have been prepared in generic form for use in the U.S. and Canada.]

Bylaws of [name] Church

Article I. Offices

Section 1.01 Principal Office.

The principal office of [name] Church (hereafter "church") shall be located at [address]. The board of directors may change the address of the principal office. Any such change shall be noted in these bylaws, but shall not constitute an amendment to these bylaws.

Article II. Members

Section 2.01 Eligibility.

There shall be one class of members, and each member shall have the same voting rights. Members may be admitted by the board of directors in its absolute discretion upon application in the form prescribed by the board.

Section 2.02 Rights and Duties.

Memberships are nonassessable. Memberships may not be assigned. The board shall maintain a record of members which shall be open to inspection by any member during normal business hours at the principal office of the church, upon five days written notice to the board stating the reason for the inspection. Members of the church shall not be liable, solely because of such membership, for the debts of the church.

Section 2.03 Termination.

Any person's membership shall terminate on the occurrence of any of the following: Voluntary resignation; death; a vote by two-thirds of the board to terminate the membership after 14 days written notice to the member of the board's intention to so act. The board shall adopt and publish to the members a policy regarding termination of memberships which shall be followed until amended by the board, which amendments shall be published to the membership ten days prior to use of any changed provisions. Publication to the membership shall be in writing, distributed at a regular worship service or mailed to all members by first class mail.

Section 2.04 Meetings.

Meetings of the members shall be held at the principal office of the church or at the place of its regular worship services. The members shall meet annually, in the first quarter of each year at a time set by the board and published, as set out above, to the members two weeks prior to the meeting, for purposes of electing directors and transacting such other business as may properly come before the meeting. Special meetings of the members shall be called by the board upon written request by five percent or more of the members for the purposes set out in such request. Notice of such special meetings shall be sent by first class mail to all members two weeks prior to such meeting, and within seven days of receipt of the written request for such meeting. Notice of a meeting may be waived in a writing signed by all members. All persons entitled to vote at the time meeting notices are sent shall be entitled to vote at such meeting unless they have died or voluntarily resigned.

Section 2.05 Notices.

Notices to members shall be in writing and mailed by first class mail to the address shown on the church roll, unless other methods of notice are provided in these bylaws. The notice shall include the date, place and time of the meeting, list those matters to come before the meeting, and name nominees for offices where appropriate. Mailed notice is deemed given when mailed. The transactions of any meeting, however called or noticed, shall be valid if, either before or after the meeting, all persons entitled to vote at the meeting sign a written waiver of notice, consent to holding of the meeting, and a copy of the minutes of the meeting.

membership

meeting notifications

Section 2.06 Quorum.

Those persons present at a duly noticed meeting of the members constitute a quorum for the transaction of business. The quorum shall not be lost by the withdrawal of members prior to adjournment. Any meeting may be adjourned by a majority vote of those members present. Each member has one vote. There shall be no proxies.

Section 2.07 Ballots.

Election of directors shall be by written ballot. Any other vote may be by written ballot at the discretion of the chairperson.

[Congregations wishing to operate by consensus may certainly do so. It is suggested that voting provisions be retained in the bylaws, perhaps simply stating that written ballots may be used at the discretion of the chairperson. Not providing any method for breaking a deadlock in the event of a failed consensus can have bad results. Most jurisdictions provide for dissolution of a deadlocked corporation upon application of a member. If your bylaws provide no method for breaking the deadlock, you could quickly be out of business. A church planting situation where people have no history of consensus needs secondary provisions in its bylaws. Unless the bylaws state differently, all jurisdictions provide for decision making by majority vote.]

Section 2.08 Conduct of Meetings.

The chairperson of the board shall preside at meetings of the members. In that person's absence, the board shall appoint another person to preside. The secretary of the board shall act as secretary of all meetings of members. In the secretary's absence, the chairperson of the meeting shall appoint a substitute. Robert's Rules of Order as amended from time to time shall govern the meetings of members to the extent they do not conflict with the Articles of Incorporation, these bylaws or law. The chairperson shall appoint tellers to receive and count ballot votes at any meeting of members.

(As with the discussion of voting above, not stating that Robert's Rules of Order apply leaves you open to helpless wrangling on minor procedural points. One person who knows parliamentary procedure can easily take control of a meeting away from the chairperson if there are not firm procedural rules. The other side of that problem is that without firm procedural rules, the chairperson becomes a dictator. Neither is desirable. You need not follow the rules in most cases, but when push comes to shove, they are there.)

Article III. Board of Directors

Section 3.01 The Church shall have ( ) directors.

The directors shall constitute the board of directors ("board" herein).

Section 3.02 Qualifications.

The directors shall all be members of the church. Subject to transitional provisions below, the directors shall hold office for a term of three years, and until their successor is elected. Directors may serve no more than two consecutive elective terms.

Section 3.03 Nomination.

Nomination of directors shall be in the manner prescribed by the board from time to time. The board shall provide a method by which members may nominate directors, except as provided in the transitional provisions below.

Section 3.04 Election.

Directors shall be elected at annual meetings of the church. Nominations shall be included in the notice of meeting published to members. Each member may cast one vote for one nominee for each vacancy on the board. There shall be no cumulative voting. The persons receiving the highest number of votes are elected to the board. Directors shall serve without compensation.

Section 3.05 Meetings.

A regular meeting shall be held without notice [the first Monday evening of each month at 7 p.m.] at the principal office of the church. If such regular meeting falls on a legal holiday, the meeting shall be held on the next succeeding [Monday] which is not a legal holiday. Any officer or any two directors may call a special meeting of the board by giving oral notice or written notice mailed four days prior to the time scheduled for the meeting. Such notice shall include the purpose of the meeting. The actions taken at any meeting of the directors shall be valid without notice if, either before or after the meeting, all directors sign a written waiver of notice, consent to the meeting, and the minutes of the meeting.

The chairperson of the board shall preside at meetings, or in that person's absence, the board shall designate a chairperson. A majority of the authorized number of directors constitute a quorum for the transaction of business. A majority of the directors present may adjourn a meeting to another time, with notice being given to directors not present at the time of the adjournment.

Section 3.06 Removal.

Except as provided in the transitional sections below, the board may remove a director who has been declared of unsound mind by final order of a court, has been convicted of a felony, or who has failed to attend three consecutive meetings of the board. The board may, by a vote of two-thirds or more of the other directors, remove a director without cause. Notice of intent to move for such removal must be given to all directors in writing, mailed two weeks prior to the time scheduled for the meeting.

Section 3.07 Resignation.

A director may resign by giving written notice to an officer of the church. Resignations shall be effective upon receipt, unless such resignation would leave the church with no director, in which case it shall not be effective until another director has taken office.

Section 3.08 Vacancies.

Vacancies on the board shall exist upon death, resignation or removal of a director, upon increase in the authorized number of directors, or upon the failure of the members to fill a vacancy at an annual meeting. A majority of the directors remaining in office, or the sole remaining director, may fill such vacancies, whether or not a quorum remains.

appointing committees

Section 3.08 Committees.

The board may appoint such committees from among itself and the members as may be necessary for the proper functioning of the church.

Section 3.09 Transitional Provisions.

The initial board of directors of the church shall consist of the incorporators, who need not be members, and who shall serve for terms extending to the third annual meeting of the church. At the second annual meeting of the church the members may elect three directors in the manner provided above. At the third annual meeting of the church the members may elect as many directors as there are authorized vacancies. Incorporators shall be eligible for election as directors if they are members of the church. Directors elected at the third annual meeting shall draw lots to determine which have two-year terms and which have three-year terms so that approximately one-third of the board is elected at each annual meeting.

[Note: The incorporators are the support group mentioned earlier.]

Article IV. Officers

alternate names for board of directors

Section 4.01 Number and Titles.

The officers of the church shall be chairperson, secretary, treasurer, and such other officers with such titles and duties as may be determined by the board. The chairperson is the chief executive officer of the church, and the treasurer is the chief financial officer of the church. No person may hold more than one office. The officers shall be appointed annually by the board from its members, and may be changed at the pleasure of the board.

Section 4.02 Duties of the Chairperson.

The chairperson shall preside at all meetings of the board or the members, and shall be the chief executive officer of the corporation, having supervision, direction and control of all its activities, subject to the control of the board. The chairperson is hereby granted the right to vote or execute a proxy to vote shares of stock, bonds, debentures or other evidences of indebtedness of other corporations held by the church. The chairperson shall have such other and further duties as may be required by law, these bylaws, the Articles, or as may be assigned by the board.

Section 4.03 Duties of the Secretary.

The secretary shall keep, or cause to be kept, at the principal office of the church minutes of the meetings of the board and the members, and shall perform such other and further duties as may be required by law, these bylaws, the Articles, or as may be assigned by the board.

Section 4.04 Duties of the Treasurer.

The treasurer shall keep adequate and accurate written books of account of the properties and business transactions of the church. The books of account shall be open to inspection by the directors at all times. The treasurer shall deposit all money and valuables received by the church in such depositaries as may be designated by the board in the name of and to the credit of the church. The treasurer shall disburse the funds of the church in accord with the instructions of the board and shall render accounts of all such transactions and the financial condition of the church to the board on a monthly basis. The treasurer shall perform such other and further duties as may be required by law, these bylaws, the Articles, or as may be assigned by the board.

Article V. Miscellaneous

Section 5.01 Amendments to the Bylaws.

These bylaws may be amended by the board at any regular or special meeting of the board, providing that notice of intention to move the amendment of the bylaws has been given in writing to all directors 14 days prior to the meeting by personal delivery or by mailing such notice by first class mail. Such notice shall include the text of the proposed amendment. All amendments to the bylaws must be presented to the members for approval or rejection at the next annual meeting, and shall be valid until rejected by the members at such meeting.

Section 5.02 Notices.

Unless otherwise stated in these bylaws, any notice may be given orally or in writing. If provision is made for mailing of notice, that notice is deemed given at the time of mailing. Mailed notices shall be sent by first class mail to the address listed for a member on the roll of the church, and shall be mailed at the post office servicing the zip or postal code of the church's principal office. Members shall give written notice of change of address to the secretary.

[End of Bylaws]

annual meeting of members

Organizational Presuppositions of the Model

These bylaws do not sound very "churchy" because they are quite similar to any corporate bylaws. There is nothing in them about deacons, Sunday school, music committee, or any of the other things we have been accustomed to seeing in church constitutions. All of those things are covered in Section 3.08 where the board is given the power to appoint "such committees as are necessary for the proper functioning of the church." This allows any type of discernment process to be used to identify gifts and maximum flexibility in organization. How strange to spend time at a church meeting discussing and voting on amendment of the bylaws just for the creation of a committee! But that is what many of us are used to.

It also seems strange to have a board of directors for a church. Of course that is what the group is no matter what they are called. You may call them the church council, or the trustees, or the elders, or anything else. A common problem in churches over the years is determining who has the authority to sign legal documents. It is common for the church council to be in charge of the business of the organization, but for the trustees to have the land in their name. So who signs a contract to build on the land? The model bylaws eliminate that sort of problem. If you want to have trustees to take care of the property, appoint them.

Where this model can go wrong is where it is used without any vision for the structure to follow it, and where no confession of faith or statement of belief is adopted. This model is the way to begin. It is not a model to impose upon an existing, traditional church, nor is it a permanent church structure. We have tended over the years to separate the business of the church from its spiritual life, leaving the work of church boards to "business" people while the "creative" or "spiritual" people operated the program. The model presented here presumes that the board will be a careful mix of people representing all aspects of the life of the church.

For example, if you have a worship ministry team whose primary task is the planning of worship, it is not reasonable to expect them to spend their meeting time examining the lease to the worship space. Yet that space is a vital aspect of their program, and they must be involved in setting the terms for its use. A member of the worship ministry team must be party to the board's discussion of lease terms; that usually means being a member of the board.

Board building is more important than we sometimes think. If you give the board interesting work to do, you will not have any trouble getting a good mix of people. If the board hears reports and discusses the financial situation, you will have difficulty filling the slots, and will find your program people fighting the board. The model provided here works best when the board is actively involved in the visioning process of the church and is made up of people involved in each area of the life of the church. Program subgroups will probably find their own members through a gift discernment process, and bring those names to the board for appointment. If no board member was involved in the visioning process which led to that slate of names, misunderstandings may develop because you have disconnected business and program. The board can only do the sort of long-range vision building which is so vital to a church when it is involved in the daily vision building of the congregation.

Board membership should be exciting!

Being a member of the board should be exciting. Responsibility for making it so rests with the pastor in most cases. Most boards will do as much or as little as their key staff people ask.

While the bylaws do not say it, only the board can hire a pastor under this model. The board will certainly ask for a congregational vote or other show of support for major changes, but it is the directors who make the final decision.

Under most church constitutions it is hard to tell where final authority lies. Quite often there is some sort of throw-away line about the council (or whatever it is called) serving "subject to the members." What does that mean? We are all accustomed to churches where the congregation as a whole either decides or ratifies certain important decisions. There is no reason why the board created under this model structure cannot list certain actions which require congregational vote.

Don't change bylaws because of previous individuals' failures.

By making the model simple (notwithstanding all the legal jargon), the board can create any kind of internal structure for the operation of the church. If a pastor-relations committee or a group to handle Sunday morning setup is needed, it is formed. If the pastor wants three weeks off, there is one place to go to ask for it. When the group no longer needs a committee, it is dissolved. These bylaws work best if they do not become cluttered. If something is so important that it has to be frozen into the bylaws, what are you saying about it? Who doesn't trust whom? What are you defending? Bylaws tend to follow on the heels of negative personal experiences. If your chairperson was a petty dictator, the bylaws are amended to strip the chairperson of power. Would it not be better to more carefully choose the next chairperson than to shackle succeeding leaders with the failings of their predecessors?

The model presupposes that all will not always be well. Disagreements on major issues will arise. By providing procedures for special meetings and notices, the model eliminates much of the danger of a snap vote on a major issue. It gives the board much power in such a situation, but allows changing one-third of the board each year. In such situations it is good to walk a line between fast action and stability. In a new congregation with no history together, the group is rather volatile to have all power reside in the congregation at first. By having three years pass before full autonomy is reached, the period of greatest volatility is passed, and the sponsoring group has some assurance that its support is being used in a way it had planned.

There is no perfect solution to this perennial dilemma. By having a board with clear authority, it is possible to make movement on issues, and it is possible to replace the board fairly rapidly if they are too far from the will of the members.

Membership is always a touchy issue. This model does what most congregations do by lodging authority over membership in the board, but does it more clearly than many congregations. It is common to see a complicated process in the bylaws for accepting and removing members. This model simply gives the board discretion to set its own procedures. If it wants to require some sort of class before full membership, that is fine. Only one class of membership is included since associate members seldom have voting rights anyway. If the church wants to have some other sort of member classification, the board can adopt it without changing the bylaws. A bylaw amendment would be needed to give voting rights to other classes of members.

Transitional Provisions

The principal transitional provision in the bylaws is Section 3.09 which describes the process by which the support group becomes the initial board and is replaced by persons directly elected by the congregation. It presumes that there will not be a congregation by the time the first annual meeting rolls around, and so waits until the second annual meeting to allow election of directors by the members. The goal is to replace the initial group at the third annual meeting, having added three new directors from the congregation the year before to give some continuity. Since part of the original group may be core group members whom the congregation would like to retain on the board, that is permitted.

This transition from a supported group to full autonomy is one which often causes difficulty. A pastor or board which tries to keep too much power will alienate those who want to participate in decision making. In a church planting where everyone is new, a longer gap between first attendance and full decision-making authority is appropriate. In a new church composed of relocated persons, it may be that no gap is appropriate. The relative initiative between sponsor and members is another variable to consider. If a group of people come together as a church, hire a pastor, and are completely self-supporting from the beginning, it is inappropriate to place any authority outside the group. Where an area regional conference employs a church planter to begin forming a church in an area where there is no core group waiting, full authority in the sponsor is appropriate. The model presented here draws a line between these two extremes. You may vary the speed of the transition, although making it longer is not advisable. As long as the congregation receives support from a sponsor, it is reasonable for the sponsor to have some representation in decision making.

No total number of directors is suggested, since that will depend to some extent on the job of the board in your developing structure. Five to six people are suggested for the original group, with a final size of around nine. Group building is important for effective board functioning, and larger size prevents that. The blank in Section 3.01 is the final number of directors you want. If you want to spread out the transition more, go ahead, but be cautious about slowing the transition so much that the members begin to think their church is controlled by outsiders.

There is divergence of opinion on whether or not board members should all be key leaders of different aspects of church program. Some congregations have the chairpersons of all committees on the board. That may not be advisable for several reasons. If creating a committee means adding a board member, you will need a bylaw amendment to do it, thus increasing the size of the board. If eliminating a committee means kicking someone off of the church board, you will never eliminate a committee. If people are only on the board because they fill a certain com-

From core group to congregation may take three annual meetings.

mittee slot, there is no room to put other gifted people on the board. If all your key program people are on the board, their energy will not be directed toward the work of the board, but at their program. You wind up with a board which meets because it has to, hears everyone's report, takes no action, and is too tired to do any visioning.

One suggestion is that you choose a board which represents all areas of church life, but which is made up of people of vision who are called together to help direct the vision building and leadership of the church. Try to create a climate where board members are chosen because of their ability to provide vision, leadership and spiritual guidance to the church. That will go a long way toward avoiding the separation of business and program, and will recognize the spiritual dimension of all the work of the church.

Dispute Resolution Methods

It should be apparent by this time that the model bylaws have many provisions designed for use when relationships within the congregation are strained. Good procedures for decision making will help in such situations, and may defuse tense situations. Conflict is often due to change. There is a well-documented cycle of conflict, described by Shawchuck, Augsburger and others. When change happens, confusion often begins. **The best conflict resolution process is one which keeps information flowing during times of change to prevent confusion from developing. Many potential conflicts can be averted by maintaining open lines of communication.**

If communication is not adequate and confusion sets in, tension will develop. Stage two of conflict begins a time of role confusion. Who is in charge here? The ability to depend on one another declines. Blaming begins. Open communication at this stage may still be adequate to end the conflict. If one side will talk openly about their perceptions at this stage, it may be possible to straighten things out. If nothing is done, the conflict moves to the next stage.

The next stage of the conflict will see people taking sides and beginning to collect injustices to use when the fight breaks out. An open structure where communication flows well is still able to resolve many conflicts at this stage by showing that the injustices are unintentional. If this stage is not interrupted by open communication, it will continue until the fight stage. Few conflicts can be stopped at this third stage without an outside mediator. This mediator only needs to be outside the conflict, not outside the group. Great negative energy is expended at this stage. There must be intervention to prevent an open fight.

The fight stage will focus on personalities instead of issues. After the fight comes the stage of adjustment. If there has been no intervention, the adjustment will be in the direction of distancing between people involved. People leave the church; spouses separate; domination is established. The fight stage can be managed by an outside mediator in a way which leads to closeness rather than distancing. Your church needs to set up a system for handling disputes at or before the grievance collecting stage. This applies to church fights and to interpersonal fights among members.

As you set up your structure, look for open structures which invite participation and sharing of concerns. As you and other key leaders relate to people, look for a feeling of openness in your relating. If someone is uncomfortable with what you do, are you open to hearing about it? It takes very little to communicate a closed mind. Having a small group of people charged with listening can help. Choose those persons who seem most open as listeners and let the congregation know they are doing that. Some established congregations have pastor support groups or deacons charged with this task. Include safe listeners in your structure. If people are not regularly coming to you with concerns, examine your ways of relating to find how you communicate a closed stance. It may be good to consult with a person experienced in group process or interpersonal relations.

Choose board members who provide vision.

Conflict is often due to change.

Develop a "listening" group.

Beyond these issues of openness, persons in the congregation gifted in mediation should be identified, and given training in dispute resolution skills. Workshops are available through Mennonite Conciliation Service, as well as a variety of other church consultants. If dispute resolution processes have visible priority in your congregation, people will presume they are to use them. Make it easy for your people to resolve their disputes. We have been given the ministry of reconciling humanity to God, and can begin doing that as we help reconcile individuals to one another. **Persons who hate their brother or sister in Christ have been separated from the love of God. We need to step into that breach.**

Looking beyond the congregation itself, the church planter and/or support group is likely to have conflict with the sponsoring group at some points. Early in your planning set up a system by which such disputes can be handled. Decide in advance who will act as mediator between you and the sponsoring group. Agree that either can go to the mediator with a concern and the mediator will then call a meeting. Rather than beating around the bush, discuss the issues for what they are—conflicts.

The earlier conflicts are addressed, the easier they will be to resolve. Where there is no method of dealing with these disputes, we may find new churches leaving the regional conference or cutting off relationships with their sponsors. Having a dispute resolution system in place allows issues to be discussed more openly. If you know you can call in a mediator, your willingness to bring up the painful subject will be greater, and the other person's willingness to listen will be greater.

As with many things, preparing for the worst may well prevent it from happening. As we take one another seriously and plan for dealing with things that come up in the normal course of being human together, we truly begin to be the church.

2. Tax Exemption

A. WHAT IT IS

There are several aspects of tax exempt status. An organization, such as your church, can be organized on a **nonprofit** basis and be exempt from paying tax on its income. That does not necessarily mean that donations to the organization will be tax deductible for a donor. For a church to qualify as a **charitable organization,** donations to which are deductible from a donor's income tax, it must qualify by filing an appropriate application with either the Internal Revenue Service (U.S.) or Revenue Canada. Deductibility of donations from state income tax is a separate issue, although an organization exempt from U.S. income tax will most likely qualify in any state. There is no provincial income tax. There are some local governments which have an income tax; these have other methods of qualifying for exemption. Yet another tax exemption issue involves local property taxes. Most places exempt from property taxation any property owned by charitable organizations. A separate application process is required for this.

B. HOW TO GET IT

Federal

In the U.S., an organization organized for religious purposes must file an Application for Recognition of Exemption under Section 501(c)(3) of the Internal Revenue Code to be recognized as tax exempt. A major exception to this for readers of this book is that the General Conference Mennonite Church has received a group exemption letter by which any of its member congregations are entitled to recognition of exemption without filing the application. A letter requesting recognition of exemption, accompanied by a letter from a denominational officer stating that the new church is a constituent congregation is all that is required. The Mennonite Church is con-

Hating others separates us from the love of God.

Apply to the I.R.S. or Revenue Canada.

29

See if your denomination has a group exemption (U.S. only).

sidering working toward a group exemption letter. Other denominations also have group exemptions. Some people tell churches they do not need to file the application since churches are automatically exempt. That is true as far as it goes. **The exemption is not recognized by the government until the formalities are taken care of. It can be embarrassing to have a potential donor ask for a copy of your exemption letter when you do not have one.**

Filing the lengthy U.S. Application for Recognition of Exemption without the help of a lawyer and/or accountant may lead to difficulties. Check with your regional conference office regarding group exemption before preparing the application. A congregation which has its exemption through a regional conference group determination letter loses its recognition of exemption if it leaves the regional conference. If you need to file the application, order the packet from the Internal Revenue Service.

Expect a letter of notification.

After filing the application or sending the letter, the Internal Revenue Service will determine whether you qualify for both tax exemption and deductibility of contributions, and send a **letter of notification.** Keep this letter with your original Articles of Incorporation and other valuable documents. The main items looked for in an application are public support and operations which seem designed for religious purposes rather than the enrichment of an individual. Obtain the application by calling the Internal Revenue Service toll-free forms number or writing to your nearest Internal Revenue Service center. If you are filing the full application, you will want help from an accountant or lawyer familiar with the application.

Earned income may not be tax exempt.

Remember that donated income can be exempt from taxes, but earned income may not be. If the church operates a business for purposes of supporting programs of the church with the money earned, that income is not tax exempt. An example is Christian Brothers Winery. Income from the winery operation is given to the schools supported by Christian Brothers, but the winery itself has nothing to do with the program of the church. The winery pays income tax. Day care centers and the like may be part of the program of a church, or they may be profit-making businesses operated by the church. Don't assume. Check with an accountant.

In Canada, there is no group exemption, so each congregation must separately file an application for a Charitable Registration Number with Revenue Canada. Practically speaking, the application process is not as difficult as the U.S. version, and membership in a conference will facilitate rapid processing.

State

In each of the states which has an income tax, it is necessary for a church to apply for **recognition of exemption.** The application is much less detailed than the federal application since it asks for a copy of the federal form or for a copy of the federal determination letter. It would be possible for a state to deny the exemption while the federal government approved it. Use of the regional conference's group determination letter should also speed any state process, and may also eliminate the application. Some states have reporting requirements for charitable organizations. You will be notified when you incorporate if that is the case in your state.

waiver of sales tax for purchases

Sales tax is a state tax which is waived for churches many places. You will need to apply for a sales tax number (sometimes you just get a letter instead of a number) through your state sales tax agency. When you purchase something for the church, giving the sales tax number (or whatever) will waive the sales tax.

City

Here we are primarily concerned about property tax, although you may have a local income tax. Your accountant can help you with both. If your church owns either land or equipment, the local property tax affects you. There are filing requirements for exemptions which must be met. Check into this before you purchase property of any kind. Your county assessor is a likely source of information if you do not yet have an accountant.

3. Employment/Self-Employment Issues

Churches employ people. That means they must behave like any other employer for national and state/provincial reporting purposes. In the U.S., call the Internal Revenue Service toll-free forms number for "Federal Employment Tax Forms," a packet of everything a new employer needs, and "Circular E," which contains information about employment taxes. Also request a **Federal Employer Identification Number** using form SS-4. The Employer Identification Number is what banks ask for when you open an account, sometimes calling it your tax number. It should be one of the first things you get after incorporation. Your accountant can help you with it. In Canada, request employer tax forms from Revenue Canada.

If the congregation's person in charge of matters regarding employment is not currently an employer, they will need to learn a lot. Have that person and the pastor/church planter discuss employment issues with an accountant before hiring anyone. As soon as the support group organizes and incorporates, the pastor can be employed by the church. Before that time the pastor will be attached to a regional conference office or other sponsoring group.

If pastor(s) are licensed or ordained, they are considered self-employed in the U.S. This alters how they are handled. Talk to your accountant about these differences. In Canada, a pastor is treated like any other wage earner, having no self-employment status except under unusual circumstances. Canadian pastors do not have to include their car allowance in reported income, and housing can be provided with only an amount set by Revenue Canada audit as reasonable rental being counted as income. Check these with an accountant. Pastors must file self-employment tax returns in the U.S.   The laws relating to this area change regularly.   So, see an accountant regarding current practices.

There are a great number of ways in which the income taxes of pastors are different from other wage earners. Specialized assistance is needed in tax preparation. In choosing a tax preparer, be bold to ask about experience with tax preparation for pastors. It is a good idea to talk to other pastors in the area about the skills of tax preparers. Many pastors do their own taxes, but a beginner needs help.

Some particular areas for a U.S. pastor to be aware of are housing allowance, automobile allowance, health insurance premiums and Social Security. At present (1987 law), pastors in the U.S. are allowed to receive a housing allowance which is not included in their income for tax purposes, although it is included for Social Security purposes. The housing allowance is limited to the actual cost of housing, including mortgage interest, property taxes, rent, utilities, maintenance, etc. If the pastor purchases his/her own home and pays mortgage interest, that interest is also deductible, which gives the effect of a double deduction for a pastor who owns a home and receives a housing allowance. This double deduction is under fire and may not survive. Check with a local accountant before using any of this specific information. New for 1987 is deductibility of 25 percent of health insurance premiums for a self-employed person such as a pastor. Automobiles used for business purposes can be the source of a deduction either on a mileage basis or on the basis of actual expense including depreciation. This is also undergoing change. An automobile allowance is ordinary income.

Historically in the U.S., a pastor could decide whether or not to be part of Social Security. Most pastors chose not to be part of it. That changed in 1986. **Now pastors can only get out of Social Security tax by declaring themselves conscientiously opposed to it, and getting a letter from their denomination saying that the denomination supports that belief.** Due to historical reliance on mutual aid, Mennonites are able to qualify as conscientiously being opposed to Social Security, but the movement among Mennonite pastors seems to be that of joining social security.

Remember that your state/province may have unemployment insurance and workers' compensation insurance laws which apply to you. Check with your advisers about these matters. Whether or not the pastor is covered by these laws will vary.

Obtain a Federal Employer I.D. number.

Licensed or ordained pastors are self-employed (U.S.).

Get an accountant for tax preparation.

housing allowance

automobile allowance

exemption from Social Security

4. Banking and Accounting Issues

We have discussed many of these issues earlier. What cannot be overstressed is starting out right. It is more trouble to set your systems up correctly in the first place, but it will be much more trouble to undo an inadequate system later.

computers

Accounting by computer can be a great time saver. Many small businesses run a full general ledger system in their microcomputer. For a new church, handwritten bookkeeping will certainly be less trouble than computer bookkeeping overall, and if you have your reports prepared by an accountant's computer system, you may even have them on time and correct. If the church has a computer for word processing, having it tied up by the bookkeeper for days at a time will not be good. When you need to replace the bookkeeper, who will train the new bookkeeper in the computer system?

Nevertheless, if you have an experienced volunteer bookkeeper who wants to use a home computer, who will say no? Whichever system you use, have an accountant participate in setting it up and training the first users, as well as subsequent users.

If you want to use an integrated church computer software system, feel free to not use the accounting part of it. Just because you bought it does not mean you have to use it. Use the membership tracking and mailing list capabilities alone.

Write checks for everything.

Earlier we discussed money handling issues such as embezzlement and other problems. The key thing to remember is to double check everything. If income has to be receipted and deposited with two people present; if someone besides the check writer examines all cancelled checks and compares them to the check register; if someone besides the treasurer audits the books annually; your chances of tempting someone go down dramatically. Have all accounts handled the same way. The deacons or youth do not need a separate checking account which the treasurer doesn't see. One person writes all checks (with a backup for vacations, etc.) and two people sign all checks. Have people who are readily available do these jobs so you don't wind up circumventing the system to avoid having to get a signature from someone who is always out of town. It is best not to give cash to anyone for anything. If there is a love offering for a speaker, deposit the money and write them a check.

Find a bank that won't charge you for its services. There are some. Be careful about the signature cards. You want to have some flexibility in who signs checks, but not too much. Remember that elimination of temptation is a goal. When officers change, change the signature cards immediately. Handle your account professionally. You may want to borrow money from the bank some day.

IV—FACILITIES

1. Temporary

A. ALL ABOUT LEASES

The largest business transaction a new church handles, after hiring a pastor, is the leasing of worship and office space. Few things are more critical to the financial life of the new church than its lease. Careful work before signing can save money later. We are presuming here that the new church will lease (rent) space for worship and office rather than buy it. The uniform advice of most church planting consultants is to wait several years before buying.

There are exceptions due to local conditions. One group of consultants which disagrees and says to buy immediately is composed of those interested in planting independent churches. A church with no stable regional conference connection needs its own building to have any appearance of stability. We will discuss buying later in this chapter.

If you use real estate agents to help in your search, ask them what their fee is. There should be a written contract if they want to be paid. When you find a place to rent, it will likely be some sort of commercial building, and will have a commercial lease to be signed. There is much more to negotiate than monthly rent. You should have a general discussion with your lawyer about local lease practice before beginning any serious search for space, including some idea of monthly rent to expect.

real estate agent fees

It is not a good idea to have a person with no experience in commercial leases negotiating the terms of a commercial lease. **The negotiating team should include one knowledgeable person, even if you have to hire one.** The usual practice is for landlord and tenant to have a general discussion of the terms, and for the landlord to then prepare a written lease. The usual lease will run up to 20 pages. A shorter lease is actually more dangerous in many ways because it does not describe as many "what ifs." Leases are written with a slant toward either landlord or tenant, depending on who writes the lease. A short lease will leave out things which are in the writer's best interest to leave out. It is most common for the landlord to provide the written lease.

Landlords usually provide leases.

If you are renting a space which has not been rented before, or are renting from an inexperienced landlord, you may end up providing the lease. If that is the case, have your lawyer do it. **Do not, under any circumstances, attempt to handle writing your own lease unless you are a lawyer heavily involved in real estate.** Some landlords may want an oral month-to-month lease, most likely because they have some plan to use the building, but aren't ready to do it yet. A church which may have to move on one month's notice is not the stable group most people are looking to join.

If the church must provide the lease, get a lawyer.

There is a sample commercial lease on the following pages, accompanied by notes of explanation. This lease has been boiled down so that only those parts which are of particular importance are in detail. This lease form is not usable as a lease. It is only provided here so that you can see what I am talking about in the notes that accompany it.

THE LEASE

Who are the parties to the lease? Usually it is not difficult to identify the landlord, but you need to know that **this** landlord really has the right to rent the building. Your lawyer will know the easiest way to check that out in your area. Do check. Naming the tenant is a bit trickier. If you have followed the advice in this book, you are incorporated. That solves the problem, since the church corporation will be the tenant. If you have not incorporated, you may have difficulty. Landlords are not usually interested in renting to a group of people who are not a legal entity. Discuss the matter with your lawyer, but resist the temptation to have one or two of your core group, or worse yet the pastor, rent the facility in their own name. This will lead to trouble and heartache. If the landlord wants a commitment before you are incorporated, look into renting it month by month until the incorporation is done. Incorporation is very quick if you do what has been suggested earlier.

The landlord may want one or more individuals to guarantee the lease, since the church has no financial track record. That is reasonable, but not good for the individual(s). If the church is unable to make its payments, the **guarantors** would have to make the payments, and they could sue the church and individual members. The guarantor won't be stuck if the church is a success, so we are talking about a failed church planting. All the good intentions in the world won't help if the lease is ruining an individual financially.

It is also possible for a tenant to be liable for large amounts of money without warning. This can happen if there is an injury not covered by insurance, or in the event of a natural disaster. The tenant's guarantor would be stuck in those cases as well. Try to avoid having an individual guarantee your lease. If a guarantor is needed, check with your regional conference. The support group, which includes conference representation, needs to be in on a decision to lease anyway.

CAUTION: Only a lawyer admitted to practice in your area can properly advise you on the legal effect of any lease provision. Here is what to look for and consider when negotiating. Ask your lawyer to explain the effect of your particular lease and situation.

Notes to Illustrative Church Building Lease

Paragraph 1 of the lease form describes what is being leased. Check this carefully. You may think you are getting use of a parking lot, or something else, when the landlord does not own it.

Paragraph 2 is the lease term. Be realistic about how long you want to be tied to this space. It is better to have a short term with several options to extend than to be locked in for five years. You don't know whether the project will work, or how well. Being saddled with an inadequate facility will strangle your growth. It is likely your needs will change faster than you expect in the beginning. Things you didn't notice may turn into real problems. I suggest a one-year term with a number of options to extend for an additional year.

Paragraph 3 talks about options to extend the lease. These are very important, partly so you have the choice to stay, and partly because the terms of the lease remain fixed.

Paragraph 4 provides for raising the rent for the option periods if inflation raises the cost of living. Note that it does not lower the rent in case the cost of living goes down. In a depression or recession your rent would not decrease. Negotiate an increase or decrease.

Paragraph 5 states the total rent for the lease term. You are responsible for the whole amount, not just the months you are there if the project closes.

Paragraph 6 says the landlord is not responsible for what you do.

ILLUSTRATIVE CHURCH BUILDING LEASE

THIS LEASE is made (date), between (Name), Landlord, whose address is (address), and (name), Tenant, whose address is (address), who agree as follows:

This lease is made with reference to the following facts and objectives:

(1) Landlord is the owner of the premises described in Attachment A which is commonly known as (address), and which consists generally of a store building with space for parking.

(2) Tenant is willing to lease the premises from Landlord pursuant to the provisions stated in this lease.

(3) Tenant wishes to lease the premises for purposes of operating a church.

(4) Tenant has examined the premises and is fully informed of their condition.

1. Landlord leases to Tenant and Tenant leases from Landlord the real property located in (town and state or province), described in Attachment A, and the building and other improvements located on the real property known hereafter as the premises; Tenant shall have full and unimpaired access to the premises at all times, except as otherwise provided herein.

2. The term shall commence (date), and shall expire (date).

3. Tenant is given the option to extend the term on all the provisions contained in this lease, except for the monthly rent, for (number) additional three-year periods ("extended term") following expiration of the initial term, by giving notice of exercise of the option ("option notice") to Landlord at least six (6) months, but not more than one (1) year before the expiration of the term. Provided that, if Tenant is in default on the date of giving the option notice, the option notice shall be totally ineffective, or if Tenant is in default on the date the extended term is to commence, the extended term shall not commence, and this lease shall expire at the end of the initial term.

4. Minimum monthly rent for the extended term shall be set in the following manner:

The Consumer Price Index (all items) for the United States, published by the United States Department of Labor, Bureau of Labor Statistics ("Index"), which is published for the month nearest the date of the commencement of the extended term ("Extension Index"), shall be compared with the Index published for the month immediately preceding the month in which the term commences ("Beginning Index").

If the Extension Index has increased over the Beginning Index, the monthly rent payable during the extended term shall be set by multiplying the average current monthly rent by a fraction, the numerator of which is the Extension Index and the denominator of which is the Beginning Index. As soon as the monthly rent for the extended term is set, Landlord shall give Tenant notice of the amount of monthly rent for the extended term.

If the Index is changed so that the base year differs from that used as of the month immediately preceding the month in which the term commences, the Index shall be converted in accordance with the conversion factor published by the United States Department of Labor, Bureau of Labor Statistics (or Canadian equivalent). If the Index is discontinued or revised during the term, such other government index or computation with which it is replaced shall be used in order to obtain substantially the same result as would be obtained if the Index had not been discontinued or revised.

Tenant shall have no right to extend the term beyond the extended term.

5. The rent under this lease shall be the sum of ($), payable in equal monthly installments of ($) in advance on the first of each and every month beginning (date), and continuing until paid.

6. Landlord shall not become or be deemed a partner or a joint venturer with Tenant by reason of the provisions of this Lease.

THE LEASE

Paragraph 7 may vary, but expect to pay first and last month's rent, as well as a deposit equal to at least one month's rent. This is negotiable.

Paragraph 8 applies in areas where there is a tax on business equipment. You will be liable for this tax unless you obtain an exemption. Check with your accountant.

Paragraph 9 states that if the landlord's property tax goes up, you pay the increase. This can certainly be negotiated out of the lease.

Paragraph 10 explains that you will need some sort of zoning permit to have a church in this place. Some cities have no zone for churches, and each one needs to get its own **"conditional use permit."** Negotiate a provision saying the lease is dead if the local government won't permit a church to meet there. It may take a while to find out. If you lease the building with no escape provisions, you are stuck if the local government says no. Talk to your lawyer about this.

The other big item hidden in paragraph 10 is the requirement that you pay for any government-required alterations. There will be some. Fire codes, structural codes and other governmental requirements can drastically increase the cost of preparing the building for use. You could be required to cut new doors in brick walls, install a sprinkler system, etc. Insert an escape clause which puts a limit on the amount you have to spend before being able to get out of the lease, and how that expense can be calculated in advance. Have an architect and a structural engineer advise you on what to expect by way of government requirements. Expect to pay these professional advisers.

Did you notice the sections forbidding the use of loudspeakers that can be heard outside the premises? Check out what that means and insert a clause noting that you will be using a public address system, but that it will not be an unreasonable annoyance to the neighbors. What about the prohibition on sleeping or cooking in the building? I doubt that that is okay with you. Have it taken out.

Paragraph 11. Look very carefully at **what the landlord is to maintain.** Think about what is left. Do you need to negotiate any additions to the list?

Paragraph 12. This standard clause can give a church great difficulty. It says that **the landlord has 30 days after notice to begin repairs,** unless it is a hazard. If the landlord does not do it, you do it and ask for payment. If the landlord doesn't pay, your only recourse is to sue. If you withhold rent, you are in default and can be evicted, even though the landlord was in the wrong by not paying you. This one is hard to negotiate out of the lease, and something needs to be said about reasonable time for repairs. Talk to your lawyer about local practice. As you can see, the type of landlord you have is very important. Try to choose wisely.

Paragraph 13. You maintain the interior, including any improvements you make. The improvements belong to the landlord, and you have to maintain them. The landlord can demand painting, etc., if you don't do it when it needs it. Your deposit is on the line for this maintenance.

Paragraph 14. Be careful about making changes to the building, including interior partitions. The long list of conditions is left out of this form, but you need to comply with the list in your lease.

36

7. Payment of deposit, first and last months' rent.

8. Payment by Tenant of taxes on Tenant's personal property.

9. Landlord shall pay real property tax on the premises in an amount equal to the real property tax levied on the premises for the (year) tax year ("base year"). Tenant shall pay any increase in real property tax assessed against the premises over the amount of the taxes levied against the premises in the base year.

10. Tenant shall use the premises for a church, and for no other use without Landlord's consent. Landlord shall not unreasonably withhold Landlord's consent to a change in use.

Tenant shall comply with all laws concerning the premises or Tenant's use of the premises, including, without limitation, the obligation at Tenant's cost to alter, maintain or restore the premises in compliance and conformity with all laws relating to the condition, use or occupancy of the premises during the term.

Except that Tenant shall not be obligated to comply with any law that requires alterations, maintenance or restoration to the premises unless the alterations, maintenance or restoration are required as a result of Tenant's particular and specific use of the premises at the time. Landlord shall make any alterations, maintenance or restoration to the premises required by such laws that Tenant is not obligated to make.

Tenant shall not use the premises in any manner that will constitute waste, nuisance or unreasonable annoyance (including, without limitation, the use of loudspeakers or sound or light apparatus that can be heard or seen outside the premises) to owners or occupants of adjacent properties.

Tenant shall not use the premises for sleeping, washing clothes, cooking, or the preparation, manufacture or mixing of anything that might emit any odor or objectionable noises or lights onto adjacent properties.

Tenant shall not do anything on the premises that will cause damage to the premises.

11. Except as provided elsewhere in this Lease, Landlord at its cost shall maintain, in good condition, the following:

(a) The structural parts of the building and other improvements that are a part of the premises, which structural parts include only the foundations, bearing and exterior walls (excluding glass and doors), sub-flooring and roof (excluding skylights);

(b) The unexposed electrical, plumbing and sewage systems, including, without limitation, those portions of the systems lying outside the premises;

(c) Window frames, gutters and downspouts on the building and other improvements that are a part of the premises; and

(d) Heating, ventilating and air-conditioning system servicing the premises.

Landlord shall repair the premises if they are damaged by (1) causes outside the premises over which Tenant has no control; (2) acts or omissions of Landlord, or its authorized representatives; or (3) Landlord's failure to perform its obligations under this paragraph.

12. Landlord shall have thirty (30) days after notice from Tenant to commence to perform its obligations under paragraph 11, except that Landlord shall perform its obligations immediately if the nature of the problem presents a hazard or emergency. If Landlord does not perform its obligations within the time limitations in this paragraph, Tenant can perform the obligations and have the right to be reimbursed for the sum it actually expends in the performance of Landlord's obligations. If Landlord does not reimburse Tenant within thirty (30) days after demand from Tenant, Tenant's sole remedy shall be to institute suit against Landlord, and Tenant shall not have the right to withhold from future rent the sums Tenant has expended.

13. Tenant shall, at its cost, maintain the interior of the premises, including any of Tenant's changes or alterations to the structure.

14. Except as provided, Tenant shall not make any structural or exterior alterations to the premises without Landlord's consent. Tenant at its cost shall have the right to make, without Landlord's consent, nonstructural alterations to the interior of the premises that Tenant requires in order to conduct its business on the premises. In making any alterations that Tenant has a right to make, Tenant shall comply with the following: (a long list).   All alterations made shall remain on and be surrendered with the premises on expiration or termination of the term.

THE LEASE

Notes

Paragraph 15. If you have something done by a contractor of any kind, they can file a mechanic's lien against the building. The lease says you are to keep mechanics' liens off the building. If you do not pay a contractor, you violate your lease, even if you have a disagreement with the contractor. Read the clauses in your lease carefully and be sure you have the right to contest mechanics' liens.

Paragraph 16. Check carefully what utilities you pay for, and find out what services such as trash collection cost. You may want to negotiate a change.

Paragraph 17. If the building collapses and injures people or things, and the landlord had no reason to suspect the problem, the landlord is not liable.

Paragraph 18. If someone is injured on the property, and it is not because of any fault on the landlord's part, the injured party will sue both you and the landlord, and you have to pay to defend the landlord. Your liability insurance will do this if it is written correctly, so make sure it is. The landlord should be an "additional insured" (or whatever term your company uses) on your policy.

Paragraph 19. Liability insurance is very important and must be correctly written. Your regional conference can steer you to church-related insurers. If you use a commercial insurer, shop around. A helpful agent is important and can save you money. Show the agent the lease so that its requirements are followed. You may be able to negotiate lower limits of coverage.

Negotiate to eliminate the clause about raising insurance coverages.

Note the plate glass clause. Do you have plate glass in the building? It is very expensive.

38

Illustrative Church Building Lease, continued

15. Tenant shall pay all costs for construction done by it or caused to be done by it on the premises as permitted by this lease. Tenant shall keep the premises free and clear of all mechanics' liens resulting from construction done by or for Tenant.

16. Tenant shall make all arrangements for and pay for all utilities and services furnished to or used by it, including, without limitation, gas, electricity, water, telephone service and trash collection, and for all connection charges.

17. Landlord shall not be liable to Tenant for any damage to Tenant or Tenant's property from any cause. Tenant waives all claims against Landlord for damage to person or property arising for any reason, except that Landlord shall be liable to Tenant for damage to Tenant resulting from the acts or omissions of Landlord or its authorized representatives.

18. Tenant shall hold Landlord harmless from all damages arising out of any damage to any person or property occurring in, on or about the premises, except that Landlord shall be liable to Tenant for damage resulting from the acts or omissions of Landlord or its authorized representatives. Landlord shall hold Tenant harmless from all damages arising out of any such damage. A party's obligation under this paragraph to indemnify and hold the other party harmless shall be limited to the sum that exceeds the amount of insurance proceeds, if any, received by the party being indemnified.

19. Tenant at its cost shall maintain public liability and property damage insurance with liability limits of not less than $100,000 per person and $300,000 per occurrence, and property damage limits of not less than $50,000 per occurrence.

All public liability insurance and property damage insurance shall insure performance by Tenant of the indemnity provisions of paragraph 18. Both parties shall be named as coinsureds, and the policy shall contain cross-liability endorsements.

Not more frequently than each three (3) years, if, in the opinion of Landlord's lender or of the insurance broker retained by Landlord, the amount of public liability and property damage insurance coverage at that time is not adequate, Tenant shall increase the insurance coverage as required by either Landlord's lender or Landlord's insurance broker.

Tenant at its cost shall maintain on all its personal property Tenant's improvements and alterations, in, on or about the premises, a policy of standard fire and extended coverage insurance, with vandalism and malicious mischief endorsements, to the extent of at least 100 percent of their full replacement value. The proceeds from any such policy shall be used by Tenant for the replacement of personal property or the restoration of Tenant's improvements or alterations.

It is contemplated by the Landlord and Tenant that no plate glass insurance will be obtained by either party. The parties agree that in the event plate glass on the front of the premises is broken by vandalism or burglary or similar occurrence, they will share equally the cost of replacement of said plate glass. Tenant is responsible for replacement of plate glass broken through Tenant's own fault, and Landlord is responsible for replacement of plate glass broken through any structural fault of the premises.

Landlord at its cost shall maintain on the building and other improvements that are a part of the premises a policy of standard fire and extended coverage insurance, with vandalism and malicious mischief endorsements, to the extent of at least full replacement value. Tenant shall at its cost maintain on Tenant's improvements and Tenant's property within the premises a policy of standard fire and extended coverage insurance, with vandalism and malicious mischief endorsements, to the extent of at least full replacement value. Each policy shall be issued in the name of Landlord or Tenant for the policy purchased by each. In case this lease is terminated, the insurance policy and all rights under it or the insurance proceeds shall be assigned to Landlord at Landlord's election. If Tenant fails to pay insurance premiums on policies purchased pursuant to the above paragraph when they become due, Landlord may at Landlord's election pay such premiums and Tenant shall immediately reimburse Landlord for any sum so expended.

Not more frequently than once every three (3) years, either party shall have the right to notify the other party that it elects to have the replacement value of the premises or improvements redetermined by an insurance company.

THE LEASE

Notes

Paragraph 20 says to insure yourself. The other side owes nothing to you if something goes wrong.

Paragraph 21 is important if you have a fire, earthquake or other **serious damage to the building.** Find out how long you will be stuck if the landlord decides to repair the place, and how you can get out of it. You have to take care of your own improvements; so if the landlord makes repairs, you must restore your improvements.

Paragraph 22. Termination of the lease upon condemnation by government authority is in the landlord's best interest.

Paragraph 23. When you decide to let another group use your facilities part of the time, or have a day care center, etc., the landlord has to approve this **sub-lease.** If you plan to do this, write the permission into the lease.

Paragraph 24. If you get into financial trouble, the lease could terminate.

Paragraph 25 gives a list of ways you can lose your space. Read it carefully. Negotiate to eliminate any parts in the lease which are inappropriate.

20. The parties release each other, and their respective authorized representatives, from any claims for damage to any person or the premises and to the fixtures, personal property, Tenant's improvements and alterations of either Landlord or Tenant in or on the premises that are caused by or result from risks insured against under any insurance policies carried by the parties and in force at the time of any such damage.

21. If, during the term, the premises are totally or partially destroyed from any cause, rendering the premises totally or partially inaccessible or unusable, Landlord shall restore the premises to substantially the same condition as they were immediately before destruction, if the restoration can be made under the existing laws and can be completed within ninety (90) working days after the date of the destruction. Such destruction shall not terminate the lease.

If the restoration cannot be made in the time stated in this paragraph, then within fifteen (15) days after the parties determine that the restoration cannot be made in the time stated in this paragraph, Tenant can terminate this lease immediately by giving notice to Landlord. If Tenant fails to terminate this lease and if restoration is permitted under the existing laws, Landlord, at its election, can either terminate this lease or restore the premises within a reasonable time and this lease shall continue in full force and effect. If the existing laws do not permit the restoration, either party can terminate this lease immediately by giving notice to the other party.

Landlord shall not be responsible for the repair and replacement of Tenant's improvements to the premises. Under paragraph 19 above, Tenant is required to insure Tenant's improvements to the premises. In the event of the destruction of the premises as given in the paragraph immediately preceding, if Landlord elects to restore the premises, Tenant shall be obligated to restore Tenant's improvements to the premises. If under the paragraph immediately preceding, Landlord elects to terminate the lease, or Tenant exercises Tenant's right of termination of the lease following total or partial destruction of the premises, Tenant shall pay to Landlord the proceeds received from insurance carried by Tenant on Tenant's improvements to the premises.

For purposes of the immediate preceding paragraphs regarding destruction of the premises, total destruction shall be defined as damage to the premises which would require over one-third (1/3) of the fair market value of the premises to restore.

22. In the event that the premises are condemned by a public entity, this lease shall terminate.

23. Prior to execution of any sub-lease, Landlord shall have the right to approve such sub-lessee, but Landlord shall not unreasonably withhold Landlord's approval.

24. No interest of Tenant in this lease shall be assignable by operation of law (including, without limitation, the transfer of this lease by testacy or intestacy). Each of the following acts shall be considered an involuntary assignment: (a) If Tenant is or becomes bankrupt or insolvent; (b) If a writ of attachment or execution is levied on this lease; (c) If, in any proceeding or action to which Tenant is a party, a receiver is appointed with authority to take possession of the premises.

An involuntary assignment shall constitute a default by Tenant, and Landlord shall have the right to elect to terminate this lease.

25. The occurrence of any of the following shall constitute a default by Tenant: (a) Failure to pay rent when due, if the failure continues for five (5) days after notice has been given to Tenant; (b) Abandonment and vacation of the premises (failure to occupy and operate the premises for ten (10) consecutive days shall be deemed an abandonment and vacation); (c) Failure to perform any other provision of this lease if the failure to perform is not cured within thirty (30) days after notice has been given to Tenant. If the default cannot reasonably be cured within thirty (30) days, Tenant shall not be in default of this lease if Tenant commences to cure the default within the thirty-day (30-day) period and diligently and in good faith continues to cure the default.

Notices given under this paragraph shall specify the alleged default and the applicable lease provisions, and shall demand that Tenant perform the provisions of this lease or pay the rent that is in arrears, as the case may be, within the applicable period of time, or quit the premises. No such notice shall be deemed a forfeiture or a termination of this lease unless Landlord so elects in the notice.

THE LEASE

Notes

Paragraph 26. If you don't pay rent or other charges, the landlord can rent to someone else for less and sue you for the difference, or rent it for more and evict you.

Paragraph 27. Signs are important to a new church. Make sure your lease does not have this provision. You will have to comply with city code, but you want a sign at a right angle to the building in many cases. The landlord's right to approve signs makes more sense if the landlord owns adjacent buildings.

Paragraph 28 describes when and for what reason the landlord can enter your premises. How will your church look with a "For Sale" sign on the front? Negotiate provisions more appropriate for your situation. This paragraph says the landlord doesn't owe you anything, even if these things disrupt your use of the place.

26. Landlord shall have the following remedies if Tenant commits a default. These remedies are not exclusive; they are cumulative in addition to any remedies now or later allowed by law.

Landlord can continue this lease in full force and effect, and the lease will continue in effect as long as Landlord does not terminate Tenant's right to possession, and Landlord shall have the right to collect rent when due. During the period Tenant is in default, Landlord can enter the premises and relet them, or any part of them, to third parties for Tenant's account. Tenant shall be liable immediately to Landlord for all costs Landlord incurs in reletting the premises, including, without limitation, brokers' commissions, expenses of remodeling the premises required by the reletting, and like costs. Reletting can be for a period shorter or longer than the remaining term of this lease. Tenant shall pay to Landlord the rent due under this lease on the dates the rent is due, less the rent Landlord receives from any reletting. No act by Landlord allowed by this paragraph shall terminate this lease unless Landlord notifies Tenant that Landlord elects to terminate this lease. After Tenant's default and for as long as Landlord does not terminate Tenant's right to possession of the premises, if Tenant obtains Landlord's consent, Tenant shall have the right to assign or sublet its interest in this lease, but Tenant shall not be released from liability. Landlord's consent to a proposed assignment or subletting shall not be unreasonably withheld.

Landlord can terminate Tenant's right to possession of the premises at any time. No act by Landlord other than giving notice to Tenant shall terminate this lease. Acts of maintenance, efforts to relet the premises, or the appointment of a receiver on Landlord's initiative to protect Landlord's interest under this lease shall not constitute a termination of Tenant's right to possession. On termination, Landlord has the right to recover from Tenant:

(a) The worth, at the time of the award, of the unpaid rent that had been earned at the time of termination of this lease;

(b) The worth, at the time of the award, of the amount by which the unpaid rent that would have been earned after the date of termination of this lease until the time of award exceeds the amount of the loss of rent that Tenant proves could have been reasonably avoided;

(c) The worth, at the time of the award, of the amount by which the unpaid rent for the balance of the term after the time of award exceeds the amount of the loss of rent that Tenant proves could have been reasonably avoided; and

(d) Any other amount, and court costs, necessary to compensate Landlord for all detriment proximately caused by Tenant's default.

"The worth, at the time of the award," as used in "a" and "b" of this paragraph, is to be computed by allowing interest at the rate of seven (7) percent per annum. "The worth, at the time of the award," as referred to in "c" of this paragraph, is to be computed by discounting the amount at the discount rate of the Federal Reserve Bank of San Francisco (Calif.) at the time of the award, plus one (1) percent.

Landlord, at any time after Tenant commits a default, can cure the default at Tenant's cost. If Landlord at any time, by reason of Tenant's default, pays any sum or does any act that requires the payment of any sum, the sum paid by Landlord shall be due immediately from Tenant to Landlord at the time the sum is paid, and if paid at a later date shall bear interest at the rate of seven (7) percent per annum from the date the sum is paid by Landlord until Landlord is reimbursed by Tenant. The sum, together with interest on it, shall be additional rent.

Rent not paid when due shall bear interest at the rate of (percent) per annum from the date due until paid.

27. Tenant shall have the right to place signs on the exterior of the building at its sole cost and expense. No such sign shall protrude at a right angle to the building and any sign shall follow the City Code. Landlord shall have the right of prior approval of any sign to be placed on the building by Tenant, but Landlord shall not unreasonably withhold Landlord's approval.

28. Landlord, and its authorized representatives, shall have the right to enter the premises at all reasonable times for any of the following purposes:

(a) To determine whether the premises are in good condition and whether Tenant is complying with its obligations under this lease;

(b) To do any necessary maintenance and to make any restoration to the premises that Landlord has the right or obligation to perform;

(c) To serve, post or keep posted any notices required or allowed under the provisions of this lease;

THE LEASE

Notes

Paragraph 29. Be sure you keep an **updated office address** with the landlord; it should be a place where a knowledgeable person checks the mail.

Paragraph 30. Just because the landlord did not make you pay on time this month, you can't make the landlord wait next time. **The landlord must give you written permission to do anything not spelled out in the lease.** Always get every promise in writing and send a letter "confirming" every discussion with the landlord.

Paragraphs 31-32. To show you have no ownership interest in the building, **you don't record the lease with the county recorder** (or equivalent government office), and you **do sign a deed at the end of the lease** to show that whatever interest you may have had belongs to the landlord. If you are promised the building when the present tenant leaves, remember that the other tenant may have to be evicted in a lengthy court battle. It is better to rent vacant space than to rent occupied space. The other tenant may not leave when required.

Paragraph 33. The landlord can sell the building and get out of any obligations to you if the buyer signs an agreement to be liable to you. You have no say in the matter, unlike the situation of wanting to sell your interest in the lease, in which case you need the landlord's consent.

Paragraph 34. If you cause the landlord to appear in court, or the landlord causes you to appear in court, the party at fault pays attorney fees. Also, if there is a lawsuit between you and the landlord, the loser pays both attorneys' fees.

44

(d) To post "for sale" signs at any time during the term, to post "for rent" or "for lease" signs during the last three (3) months of the term, or during any period while Tenant is in default;

(e) To show the premises to prospective brokers, agents, buyers, tenants or persons interested in an exchange, at any time during the term;

(f) To shore the foundations, footings and walls of the building and other improvements that are a part of the premises and to erect scaffolding and protective barricades around and about the premises, but not so as to prevent entry to the premises, and to do any other act or thing necessary for the safety or preservation of the premises if any excavation or other construction is undertaken or is about to be undertaken on any adjacent property or nearby street. Landlord's right under this provision extends to the owner of the adjacent property on which excavation or construction is to take place and the adjacent property owner's representatives.

Landlord shall not be liable in any manner for any inconvenience, disturbance, loss of business, nuisance or other damage arising out of Landlord's entry on the premises as provided in this paragraph, except damage resulting from the acts or omissions of Landlord or its authorized representatives.

Tenant shall not be entitled to an abatement or reduction of rent if Landlord exercises any rights reserved in this paragraph.

Landlord shall conduct its activities on the premises as allowed in this paragraph in a manner that will cause the least possible inconvenience, annoyance or disturbance to Tenant.

29. Any notices, requests or demands shall be in writing and either served personally or sent by prepaid first class mail to Tenant at (address), or to Landlord at (address).

30. No delay or omission in the exercise of any right or remedy of Landlord on any default by Tenant shall impair such a right or remedy or be construed as a waiver.

The receipt and acceptance by Landlord of delinquent rent shall not constitute a waiver of any other default; it shall constitute only a waiver of timely payment for the particular rent payment involved.

No act or conduct of Landlord, including, without limitation, the acceptance of the keys to the premises, shall constitute an acceptance of the surrender of the premises by Tenant before the expiration of the term. Only a notice from Landlord to Tenant shall constitute acceptance of the surrender of the premises and accomplish a termination of the lease.

Landlord's consent to or approval of any act by Tenant requiring Landlord's consent or approval shall not be deemed to waive or render unnecessary Landlord's consent to or approval of any subsequent act by Tenant.

Any waiver by Landlord of any default must be in writing and shall not be a waiver of any other default concerning the same or any other provisions of the lease.

31. This lease shall not be recorded.

32. Tenant shall execute and deliver to Landlord on the expiration or termination of this lease, immediately on Landlord's request, a quitclaim deed to the premises, in recordable form, designating Landlord as transferee.

33. If Landlord sells or transfers all or any portion of the premises, Landlord, on consummation of the sale or transfer, shall be released from any liability thereafter accruing under this lease if Landlord's successor has assumed in writing, for the benefit of Tenant, Landlord's obligations under this lease. If any security deposit or prepaid rent has been paid by Tenant, Landlord can transfer the security deposit or prepaid rent to Landlord's successor, and on such transfer Landlord shall be discharged from any further liability in reference to the security deposit or prepaid rent.

34. If either party becomes a party to any litigation concerning this lease, the premises, or the building or other improvements in which the premises are located, by reason of any act or omission of the other party or its authorized representatives, and not by any act or omission of the party that becomes a party to that litigation or any act or omission of its authorized representatives, the party that causes the other party to become involved in the litigation shall be liable to that party for reasonable attorneys' fees and court costs incurred by it in the litigation.

THE LEASE

Caution: This lease is incomplete and not suitable for use. It is provided here solely to illustrate concepts contained in this book. No legal opinion is offered as to the suitability or legal effect of any of the provisions contained in the sample lease in any particular jurisdiction. See your attorney for assistance in preparing or interpreting any lease. The laws by which leases are interpreted vary from jurisdiction to jurisdiction.

This long section shows how much room there is for error in lease negotiation. Go over the written lease with your lawyer before signing.

Note that there is no mediation or arbitration clause. I suggest you include a paragraph which calls for mediation of disputes and binding arbitration of disputes which are not successfully mediated. That will be faster and cheaper, and avoid the situation of having to decide whether to sue. As a professional mediator, I know how valuable such a clause is. Mennonite Conciliation Service, 21 S. 12th St., Akron, PA 17501, can help you. Also available in most areas is help from the Christian Legal Society, P.O. Box 1492, Merrifield, VA 22116. They can direct you to local chapters of Christian Conciliation Service.

IN GENERAL: Be careful how you sign. Make sure your officers sign as officers, not as individuals. The chairperson of the board and secretary are usually required to sign. Check with your lawyer.

Notes

Paragraph 35. When the lease is over, you return the building with all your improvements, unless there is a written agreement otherwise. Reasonable wear and tear is permitted, but other damage must be repaired at your expense. If you don't get out on time, the next tenant can sue you for damages.

Paragraph 36. When the lease ends, you become a month-to-month tenant.

Paragraph 37. This paragraph says the landlord's heirs are bound by the lease if the landlord dies.

Paragraphs 38-43. Things need to be done on time. The lease is the whole agreement, and there are no side agreements. Everything is in writing.

Paragraph 44. The landlord is obligated to repair the air-conditioning, but you need to pay for regular maintenance, which should eliminate most repairs. Watch for this sort of thing.

Paragraph 45. Make sure "the premises" either includes driveways and parking lots, or that you have the right to use those things. The last tenant may have had a deal with the neighbor. Get your right to use these things in writing.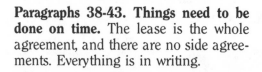

Paragraph 46. If you are renting a church building and it includes pews, etc., this paragraph will be a useful one.

Paragraph 47. Ask whether there are any potential assessment districts being discussed. You could be obligated to pay a lot of money if an assessment district goes in, and it is land **owners** who vote on them. These sorts of things are used for parking, sewers, street plantings, etc. This clause is a good one.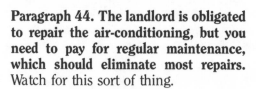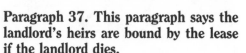

Illustrative Church Building Lease, continued

If either party commences an action against the other party arising out of or in connection with this lease, the prevailing party shall be entitled to have and recover from the losing party reasonable attorneys' fees and costs of suit.

35. On expiration of the term, Tenant shall surrender to Landlord the premises and all Tenant's improvements and alterations in good condition except for ordinary wear and tear and destruction of the premises as covered elsewhere in this lease. Tenant shall remove all of Tenant's personal property within the above stated time. Landlord can elect to retain or dispose of in any manner any alterations or Tenant's personal property that Tenant does not remove from the premises on expiration or termination of the term as allowed or required by this lease by giving at least ten (10) days' notice to Tenant. Title to any such alterations or Tenant's personal property shall vest in Landlord at the expiration of the ten (10) days. Tenant waives all claims against Landlord for any damages to Tenant resulting from Landlord's retention or disposition of any such alterations or personal property. Tenant shall be liable to Landlord for Landlord's costs for restoring, removing and disposing of any of Tenant's personal property. If Tenant fails to surrender the premises to Landlord on expiration as required by this paragraph, Tenant shall hold Landlord harmless for all damages resulting from Tenant's failure to surrender the premises, including, without limitation, claims made by a succeeding tenant resulting from Tenant's failure to surrender the premises.

36. If Tenant holds over after expiration of the term with Landlord's consent, such holding over shall be on a month-to-month tenancy terminable on thirty (30) days' notice given at any time by either party.

37. Upon Tenant's death, Tenant's personal representative shall have the option to terminate this lease within ninety (90) days of the date of Tenant's death. This lease shall be binding upon Landlord's heirs and assigns, and shall not terminate upon death of Landlord.

38. Time is of the essence of each provision of this lease.

39. This lease shall be construed and interpreted in the courts with the laws of (place).

40. This lease contains all the agreements of the parties, and cannot be amended or modified except by written agreement.

41. All provisions, whether covenants or conditions, on the part of the Tenant shall be deemed to be both covenants and conditions.

42. When required by the context of this lease, the singular shall include the plural.

43. The unenforceability, invalidity or illegality of any provision of this lease shall not render the other provisions unenforceable, invalid or illegal.

44. Tenant shall have regular air-conditioning service performed by a licensed air-conditioning service contractor no less often than twice per year at Tenant's sole expense.

45. Landlord grants to Tenant for the period of this lease a nonexclusive easement for the use of the private alley behind the premises for ingress, egress and parking. Tenant understands and agrees that this area is for the use of all of Landlord's tenants adjacent to the said private alley and that Tenant is not guaranteed any portion of the private alley for Tenant's personal use.

46. Landlord as a separate agreement hereby leases to Tenant all of the fixtures of the premises as they are existing: (terms).

47. As further consideration, Landlord shall not vote affirmatively for the creation of any assessment district without Tenant's approval if that assessment district would include the premises.

(signatures)

B. THINGS TO WATCH FOR IN SELECTING A PLACE

Is the building useable by a church?

You will want enough of the right kind of space for your goals. You will want both office and worship space. Parking is very important, as is good lighting. Ease of access and simple directions are important. Is it attractive? Is it well maintained? If you were a member of your target group, would you want to come here for church? Can you afford it? Most important, will it suit your program?

Are the landlord and neighbors easy to work with?

The items regarding the lease have covered quite a few things to watch for. A very important one is the landlord. Does this person or company take care of the place? Are they easy to work with? Do you get straight answers? What you don't want is a place that will be dark, hot or cold, and leaky. Check it out at different times of the day and in different weather if you can. Talk to the last tenant, even if that is hard to do. Talk to the neighbors. Do the neighbors want a church there? You may have trouble with the local government if the neighbors are not supportive. Check immediately with the zoning authorities to find out the situation from their perspective.

If alterations are required, don't sign the lease until you have good estimates from competent contractors and an opinion from an architect and structural engineer. That will be money well spent if you discover problems. Finally, when everything checks out, how does it feel? Is God leading you to this place?

2. Purchasing a Facility

A. A REAL ESTATE PRIMER

Real estate is land and buildings. So is "real property." The things you put in buildings are "personal property." This section has much in common with the lease discussion; we will not repeat it.

Title

Who will own this building? Once again, the corporation (or the equivalent in jurisdictions where there is no incorporation of churches) owns the property. Sometimes individuals will quickly buy a piece of land they think the church might want, planning to sell it if the congregation decides against the location. That is all right, but when the time comes, they sell it to the church (or give it).

Reversionary clauses

Link the property to the regional conference.

Young churches are volatile. They can grow and shrink rapidly, and leadership can change just as rapidly. One of the fears of church planters and home mission committees is that a change in leadership will suddenly change a church's regional conference loyalties, even though the regional conference has given a good deal of money to the church. Some people look for small, weak churches with the idea of moving their own group into the building by voting out the original group. One way to avoid many of these problems and dangers is to **include a paragraph in the deed to your property which states that the land will revert to the regional conference when the church ceases to be a member of the regional conference.** I recommend this to young and old churches alike. It is a good link to the regional conference which tells those who would lead a church away that it will not be so easy to do. This also serves notice on new pastors that the link to the regional conference is strong. At the very least, it will cause discussion between church leaders and the regional conference rather than having a sudden vote to withdraw. It is not so much a chain tying a congregation to the regional conference as it is a sign of mutual commitment. Ask your lawyer how to put such a reversionary clause in your deed when you are buying property. Expect your lawyer to try to talk you out of it.

Zoning

Zoning is important. As mentioned in the lease section, you will need to find out whether a particular property can be used for a church. Have your lawyer check it out, and do so before buying. Check sign ordinances at the same time.

B. SITE SELECTION

Zoning is one of the things included in selecting a site, but other things can also make a big difference. How far is it to sewer, water and electric connections? Bringing any of those very far is expensive. What city services are available at the site? Is this inside the city or outside? Many cities have islands of property which have never been annexed into the city. That means police and fire protection are handled differently. Regulations on parking lot size will vary depending upon zoning and other factors.

Size is an important consideration. **A common rule of thumb is one acre for each 100 members.** This is actually not much land if you have any programs in mind beyond the usual. Christian education. In city areas you may have to take less land to get any, while in suburban and rural settings land may be plentiful. Those interested in larger programs and continued growth recommend buying ten acres, planning to split off and sell some if the program develops in a way which does not use all the land.

Visibility of the land is very important. People are more likely to come to a building they see frequently. A heavily traveled street in a residential neighborhood, with nearby freeway(s) and arterial street access is what an urban church looks for. If you have to draw a map for people to find the church, they won't be as likely to come.

C. FINANCING

Borrowing money to buy land and buildings is different from a lease because the value of the land supports the loan. There should not need to be a personal guarantee for the loan. However, if you have a small down payment, or there is some question about the value of the land, the lender may require a personal guarantee. Before borrowing from a commercial lender, check with your regional conference regarding church-related lenders. Insurance companies and mission agencies all lend money. You may be able to borrow a large down payment from a church agency to facilitate obtaining a commercial loan for the rest. If you cannot get a loan for the property without a personal guarantee, something is wrong. Either the property is not worth what you are paying or there is something else you don't know about. Find out what the mystery is or forget the property.

Be slow to get commercial loans. Remember that any substantial loan will require a **deed of trust** (or mortgage) which uses the property to secure payment of the loan. If you don't make payments, the property is taken and sold for what is owed. This is a foreclosure, and it does happen to churches. Once you take out a mortgage, any other lender will be behind the first mortgage holder in line for money, and so will want higher interest for the greater risk. Church lending agencies usually want the first mortgage, since their interest is low.

How much can you afford? Talk to your regional conference officers about your situation. They will have an idea of what is reasonable in your area. Practically speaking, a loan which requires membership growth to support it is a bad idea. The stable group which seeks the loan should be able to pay it back. Visitors can tell when a church needs new givers to support a mortgage. Overbuilding can stop your growth, particularly as program dollars disappear into loan payments. Program, not debt, draws people. Careful, long-range planning needs to precede building. Nevertheless, too small facilities also stop growth. A worship space which is 80 percent full

BUILDING A WORSHIP SPACE

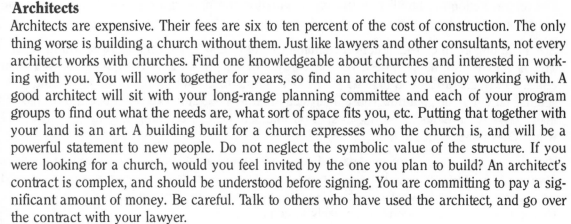

Over-building?

is completely full in the eyes of a visitor. **Overbuilding** does not mean building more space than you currently need; it means building more space than you can pay for. There are many examples of churches which violate this principle by purposely overbuilding to encourage growth. Some succeed; others don't. Carefully consider what overbuilding means for you.

The decision to leave rented space and buy or build is a major one. If the rented space is working, and the church is growing, pouring energy and money into a building may not be the best thing for the church.

D. BUILDING

Architects

Architects are expensive. Their fees are six to ten percent of the cost of construction. The only thing worse is building a church without them. Just like lawyers and other consultants, not every architect works with churches. Find one knowledgeable about churches and interested in working with you. You will work together for years, so find an architect you enjoy working with. A good architect will sit with your long-range planning committee and each of your program groups to find out what the needs are, what sort of space fits you, etc. Putting that together with your land is an art. A building built for a church expresses who the church is, and will be a powerful statement to new people. Do not neglect the symbolic value of the structure. If you were looking for a church, would you feel invited by the one you plan to build? An architect's contract is complex, and should be understood before signing. You are committing to pay a significant amount of money. Be careful. Talk to others who have used the architect, and go over the contract with your lawyer.

Other Planning Resources

Seek church consultants.

There are a variety of church consultants who advertise in church magazines. If you are interested, ask for their promotional material. Depending on the complexity of your situation and where you are located, they may be helpful. Check with regional conference staff to find out who has been used in your area, so you can ask about their usefulness. You may need to call in other experts to assist the architect. Usually the architect will take care of that at your expense. Soil engineers, structural engineers, electrical and mechanical engineers can all find a place in your planning. The more interesting your plans, the more difficult they will be to achieve. Don't forget landscaping and paving contractors.

Things to Watch For

Government agencies are a source of building difficulties. Make friends with them early in the project and work closely with them. The local planning department can hold your project hostage for a long time if they are not happy. It is a good idea to have a chat with the planning director of your town/city to indicate who you intend to use as architect and general contractor. They will let you know if those people get along well with the city staff. A contractor on good terms with building inspectors makes much faster progress than one who always argues with them.

contractors

Contractors have reputations. Find out about the reputation of your contractor before you sign a contract. Get a written contract and have your lawyer go over it. Get everything you agree to in writing. Some things are covered by the contract price and others are extras. Every time you change something, find out whether it will be extra.

using volunteer help

Some contracts are so much per square foot; others are by the job; others are by time and materials. It is advisable not to pay by time and materials, even though that will more easily allow volunteers to help. A time and materials job goes 100 percent over budget faster than you can blink. That is because every member of the church will want at least one thing changed, and the contractor will be happy to oblige. Volunteers may or may not lower the cost. Make a deal with the contractor on the use of volunteer labor at the beginning.

Be flexible in scheduling your move from rented space. You don't want the lease to run out six months before your new building is ready, and that much delay can easily occur in a building project.

A congregation is usually able to imagine itself about three times larger than it is. If you build too early in the life of your church, you will build too small and stifle your group. This is the other side of overbuilding. If you build six times larger, you will look lost in the facility and that will drive people away. Pay careful attention to your regional conference staff as you discern whether to build and how large to build. They have seen mistakes you can learn from.

Signs

Whether your space is temporary or permanent, you will need good signs to show where it is. These will be portable in a rented facility. Inside signs are also important to make visitors feel at home. Having to ask a stranger where the washrooms are is embarrassing. Have enough signs so a complete stranger can get around easily.

Single-Use vs. Multiple-Use Facilities

The day of the sanctuary with a sloping floor and screwed-down pews is not over, but should it begin for your congregation? It takes a rather wealthy group to commit a large space to worship only. It is hard to get a sense of God's majesty in a flat, low-ceilinged room that smells like a day care center—because it is one. The mix of communal feeling and transcendence is a tough one. Your space can certainly be more than a worship space without much sacrifice. A flat floor and individual seating is all it takes. The variety of uses you want is the issue, and the line needs to be drawn somewhere. Talk to your architect about this, but also visit many other church buildings, particularly newer multiple-use ones, to see the possibilities.

versatility in seating and use

In urban areas, a new idea is for a church to buy a large building suitable for multiple tenants, and to lease out portions of the building to businesses. This allows business capital to be used in paying off the building. It may be possible to go into a joint venture with a business in buying a building. Remember that expansion possibilities are important to your growth. Signing away space you may want is always a danger. A commercial structure in an urban area may seem more accessible to your target group than a traditional church building, or it may not. Careful survey work should precede a decision to enter into such an arrangement. Some good examples exist of this sort of facility. One of the big challenges in such a venture is to keep the various uses compatible, and to avoid renting to businesses which detract from the church's image in the community.

leasing out extra space

E. BUYING PRE-OWNED PROPERTY

This discussion is much like the leasing discussion. Look at it as a place to lease, then check further on value, nature of the neighborhood, demographic trends, etc. You will also need to check things a landlord would have to maintain, such as roof and walls. Do not fail to have your architect and a structural engineer examine the building.

The danger is that in your locality a sale triggers a building code examination. Talk to the building inspector about the building before you buy it, and ask the seller to request an inspection and report by the building inspector. If you do any renovations, you will trigger this examination in any event. This is a major item. Do not fail to do this.

building code examination

Ask about restrooms for the handicapped, accessibility standards and similar matters while you are talking to the building inspector. You want a facility accessible to handicapped persons, but can you afford to make this one that way immediately? Do you want the building if you can't? An inspection by the fire marshal is a good idea as well. An electrician should examine the wiring for you. Have an insulation company do an energy audit. Get copies of the heating and electric bills. Is the plumbing adequate? Have a plumber check. A roofer should examine the roof, and a termite company should examine the whole building. You may think of other things,

accessibility for handi-capped

or your locality may have a special problem that needs checking. Water seepage or some similar problem may occur in your area. All this checking may seem like a lot of trouble, but it is not as much trouble as finding structural cracks after you own the building.

3. Utilities and Maintenance Considerations

Find out what the utilities cost. Make sure they are properly transferred to the church's name. Find out what past utility bills have been. Your use may be different, so try to estimate the expense of this facility for you. Then do an energy audit with the utility company or a private insulation contractor to determine what needs to be done, if anything, to lower utility bills in a cost-effective way.

Maintenance is a sneaky item. You can defer it only so long before something breaks. It is much cheaper to fix a leak than to replace flooring which the leak rots away. Set up a fund for maintenance as part of your budget. Keep track of what needs to be done and the date when it is noticed so deferred maintenance can be caught. Otherwise, you will go from budget year to budget year with no idea just how inadequate the maintenance budget is. Whether you are renting or buying, maintenance is a must. Make up a maintenance budget as part of your decision to buy a building. Can you afford the maintenance which will need to be done in this building?

4. Insurance

A. FIRE, THEFT, MALICIOUS MISCHIEF

As you can see from the lease discussion, you will be required to have this coverage in a lease, and may be required by a lender to have it if you are buying. These coverages come in a package available from church-related and commercial companies. Talk to your regional conference staff about available church-related coverage. Know what is covered. One thing to consider is whether fire insurance is based on actual value, replacement value or some other amount. Will you get what it costs to replace your structure? How is a partial loss handled?

B. LIABILITY

"premises liability insurance"

Liability insurance relates primarily to negligence and accidents. If you are not careful how you maintain your building, and someone falls and gets hurt because of it, your liability insurance pays the person's loss. The nice thing is that you do not have to worry about how to handle the situation. Most lenders and landlords require "premises liability" insurance. This covers the owner of the building against any claims for negligence. Do not think for one moment that you will never have a claim. **Do not be without this coverage whether you are renting or buying the building.**

professional negligence coverage for pastoral malpractice suits

A new kind of liability insurance for churches is **professional negligence coverage**. Believe it or not, pastoral malpractice is possible. There is one case currently in the courts in California, *Nally versus Grace Community Church*. The California Court of Appeals has ruled that it is possible for a pastor, and the church, to be liable for counseling malpractice. The most likely situation for this liability is a person committing suicide after counseling with the pastor, as is the situation in the Nally case. The claim would be that the pastor had a professional duty to intervene in some way to prevent the suicide, or somehow caused the person to do it. This insurance is not widely available, but it is a good idea to check into it before deciding not to have it. The danger is not that you will have to pay a claim, but that defending yourself in court will be expensive.

Workers compensation insurance is liability insurance which pays for injuries to employees on the job. Each jurisdiction has different rules about this. Ask your attorney or accountant about it. You may or may not need it for a pastor.

V—EQUIPMENT

1. Worship Furniture

The main furniture needs you have in the beginning are chairs for worshipers, pulpit/lectern, communion table/altar, perhaps a keyboard instrument and miscellaneous small tables and plant holders. There should be some way to elevate those who are speaking if the worshipers sit on a flat floor. If you want more complexity in music, you may need risers for musicians and some sort of elevated place for instrumentalists. Coat racks may be important. If you want mailboxes for your members, those need to be devised.

The largest problem is seating. If you are in a school or public assembly place, chairs will be available. If your space has some other use, you will need to buy or rent chairs. If you only have the use of the space for worship and are providing your own chairs, negotiating storage space for the chairs becomes important to avoid hauling them from a garage each week. Chairs can be rented for short- or long-term. Adequate to good folding or stacking chairs can be purchased for about the same price (if not less) as two years of rent. Compare prices in your area. Equipment rental companies will deliver and pick up chairs on a weekly basis, but that gets expensive. Examine your situation from all angles. If you are very temporary in a worship space, buying chairs may not be a good idea. The next facility may have them.

Walk through your worship service, literally, from the point of view of each participant in the service. What furnishings do you need? How will the offering be taken? Where will you put it? Do musicians stay in one place or move around? Where does the preacher sit, and on what? Where are the preacher's Bible and notes kept before, during and after the preaching? Overhead projector and screen? Where do songbooks, hats, coats, visitor register(s), name tags, worship folders, etc., go? You will need tables for people to sign in, or make name tags. Do you have literature to distribute? You need racks. Portable partitions can turn a gym into a worship space nicely. Plants are important. Can you rent them? Where do all these things go after the service? Do you have a garage, or do you need a mini-storage facility? Will banners be hung? Who makes them and how are they hung?

Everything you took for granted in your home church does not exist in your temporary space. Find someone able to take charge of setting up your worship space each week. You will need a team to set up and dismantle for each service unless you have full-time use of the space. This is a big job, even for a simple setup. A complete list of equipment and procedures is needed for setup and dismantling so someone beside the regular crew can do it. All this moving will destroy your furniture. Find someone to keep it in good repair, starting immediately. It is much easier to have full-time space, but the expense has to be both justified and possible for you.

Chairs are a major investment.

Put yourself in the parishioners' shoes.

53

The question of songbooks rather than an overhead projector is an ongoing one. An overhead projector is the mark of certain church styles, and that may make the choice for you. Practically speaking, one overhead projector and screen is less to move than enough songbooks for a sizable crowd, but having a large enough screen may be a problem, as may be the amount of light in the room. **Some people think they can save money by using an overhead transparency, but that may not be true. Songs are copyrighted. Making a transparency or photocopy without permission is a violation of copyright law. You will need to obtain permission for each song.** Some publishers sell a license for all their music; others sell one at a time. All these things need to be taken into account in deciding whether to buy or borrow songbooks, make your own songbook, or use an overhead projector. Do what is right for you, after checking the facts in your situation.

Don't steal copyrighted music!

2. Office Equipment and Supplies

If you have not purchased office equipment lately, get someone who has to help you with it. Large amounts of money can be wasted quickly in this area. Also, have a fixed office space, not portable. We did not discuss office space separately in the real estate section since these concerns are the same. It may not be best for the office to be in the pastor's home. You will have volunteer office help, and a home office is not conducive to good use of volunteers. They can't come and go at odd hours; the pastor spends too much time housecleaning and entertaining volunteers; there is no privacy for counseling; and it doesn't give a professional feeling. It also becomes too easy for the pastor to do things instead of delegating them, and to control things too tightly. Get an office separate from the pastor's (or anyone's) home, if at all possible. It should have a public and a private area, even if there is usually only one person in it.

Make an office outside **the pastor's home.**

You will need a typewriter or word processor of some sort, telephone, something to duplicate materials with, chairs, equipment stands, desks, storage cabinets and supplies.

You will be producing letters, teaching materials, worship materials, publicity materials and mailing lists, and filling out forms of various kinds. Many **computers** will not do all of these jobs well. Some computers use a typewriter-style **printer** and can be used directly as a typewriter for individual address labels, file labels, forms, etc. The computer I used to write this book cannot type directly. You will want to be able to use a typewriter or have a computer which is able to act like a typewriter. I have both a typewriter and computer. Some electronic typewriters can be hooked to computers. You may want to buy such a typewriter, as well as a computer and printer suitable for your other publishing work. Unless you have a professional secretary, you will spend too much time typing without a computer, and will turn out messy materials.

computers and word processing

Computers are a real puzzle these days. You will want to do what is called "desktop publishing" with typeset-style printouts, but that is usually too expensive for most new churches (as of early 1989). Get a computer capable of handling desktop publishing software, even if you won't be using it right away. Talk to computer sales people and to computer users before buying. The field is changing too rapidly for specific information to be included in this book. Service is seldom an issue once the unit is running, but find out how easily you can get service.

"desktop publishing"

Talk to people who use the word processing software you plan to use to find out if it will easily do the jobs you need done. There is a difference between a job that "can be done" and one which is easily done. Be sure the people who will actually use the equipment are in on the discussion.

service

Church software for computers is something to look into. This software is used to track attendance, note changes in a person's attendance pattern, automatically produce letters to visitors and repeat visitors, track giving, etc. If you are serious about visitor follow-up, not to mention keeping track of your members, this type of software can be a great help. It does mean that someone needs to type in names of all attenders and addresses of visitors. If you don't have someone to do that, then the software doesn't help. Keeping track of individual giving is also a handy part of this software. It can produce quarterly receipts and also give you solid information on cash flow. Some software can track giving to special fund drives in addition to regular giving. All church administration software is designed to produce reports. A manual system can do the same. Research shows that a person stops giving three months before they leave a church. Can your system give you early warning of a pastoral care need? See Appendix G for further information on church administration software.

church software

Mailing lists can be a major item for a church planting project. You can type a master copy and make gummed labels in the photocopier, or you can keep the list in the computer. Mailing list software is part of the church administration packages mentioned above. Envelopes can be bought with tractor feed holes, so the whole list can be addressed at the push of a button by running them through the computer. This is more expensive than sticking gummed labels on regular envelopes, but not much. Using a computer also allows automatic sorting by zip or postal code for bulk mailing. You will want to use the gummed labels for newsletters, etc. These labels can also be computer printed.

One possibility that only the computer gives you is **personalized letters.** A mail merge program (available separately or in a church administration package) prints letters and mailing list together so that individually addressed letters emerge. Most people are aware that these are computer generated, so you need to know whether they would be helpful in your situation. This is a good way to acknowledge those who come to the first service and invite them back. You could also use a form letter and accomplish the same thing. Which would be better in your setting? You will need to have some system for handling the mailing list.

personal-ized letters

The **photocopier** has transformed office work. Mimeograph machines are much cheaper to own and run, but they are inflexible and not easy for inexperienced help to use. Photo-offset machines give excellent quality and are more flexible than a mimeograph, but are more trouble than a photocopier, and less flexible. Use a photocopier for your duplicating needs, taking more complex jobs to a printer. Your **church brochure,** for instance, should be printed rather than photocopied.

photocopier vs. outside printers

In the beginning you can use a copy shop for all your printing, but that will be inconvenient in the long run. You will probably want to buy a photocopier. Do an audit of your copy needs as you begin thinking about purchasing a copier. Add up your letters, publicity, worship folders, education materials, reports, articles and copying for files, then double your top figure. This will give you a minimum to work with. Double it again to be realistic. In investigating machines, find out what level of monthly copy volume they are designed for. The new personal sized copiers are great until you need 50 copies of something. You will need hundreds of things. A relatively small desktop copier will probably serve your needs. You will want enlargement and reduction capabilities to save paper and to work with graphics. I suggest you buy a copier that uses dry toner. Liquid toner copies tend to look out of focus a day after the service person has been there. Find out whether other churches in your area have service contracts on their copiers, and with whom. Copiers always break down at the worst possible time, so have a back-up plan for making copies in an emergency.

OFFICE EQUIPMENT • SOUND SYSTEMS

Investigate service contracts.

telephone directory listing

answering machines

Buy in quantity **whenever possible.**

Calculate a cost per copy for each machine you investigate based on supplies needed and known servicing costs, including replacement of the machine in five years. Including replacement of the machine in calculating your per copy cost shows it is more economical to make more copies. An expensive copier with many features will make your cost per copy very high if you don't make many copies. You may discover that in your situation it would be best to have larger jobs (including the Sunday worship folder) done by a copy shop while you have a very small and inexpensive copier for regular use in the office. The existence of a nearby copy shop makes a difference in this calculation.

You will want a **telephone** in the public part of the office, and in the private part. You will want people to be able to use the phones as an intercom, and to put calls on hold. Some areas have call transfer by which the office phone can automatically ring at another place, such as the pastor's home. Check on the availability of different services in your area and decide which you need. Then get phones that can do those things. People used to rent phones from the phone company. You can still do that; if you are in a temporary situation, that may be best. More likely, you will buy phones from someone else. Shop around, and remember that the telephone company will not repair another company's phone. Also, check on installation prices and methods.

Find out when the closing date for the **local telephone directory** is and get your listing in it. Remember that the deadline is months before the book comes out. Put your number in the yellow pages with a note to "call for time and place of services."

Answering machines are something you probably either love or hate. Church planters have neither secretaries nor do they sit by the phone. You will need an answering machine if anyone is to locate you. It should give a brief message appropriate to the stage in the life of the congregation, and invite the caller to leave name, address and phone number. For instance, when you have set a date for the first worship service, program the machine to say something like: "Hello from Any Menno Church. Our first worship service will be held December 5 in the Roosevelt School auditorium at 11 a.m. If you have any questions about the church, a message for us, or have a pastoral care need, please give your name, address and phone number at the sound of the tone. Thanks for calling; we'll be looking for you December 5." These machines can be purchased with many different features. Purchase one which allows you to get your messages from another phone.

Office furniture can be purchased or rented. When you begin, you may be tempted to rent. For the same money over the course of a year or so, you could own the furniture. Buy reasonably attractive, lower priced furniture that matches. A desk and chair for either clerical or executive use should run $350 (U.S.) or less. A pair of swivel rockers for counseling can be found on sale at regular furniture stores. Be sure to visit a discount office supply store near you. Buy a secretarial desk large enough to hold the equipment you plan to put on it. Remember that upholstered furniture wears out faster than wood furniture.

Office supplies and desk equipment costs add up fast. It is cheaper to **buy in quantity,** but you may not be able to afford to tie up that much money. Copier paper is a good place to save by buying several case lots. Stationery is also much cheaper in larger quantities. The trouble with stationery is that you don't use much, unless you photocopy letters onto the printed letterhead for mass mailings. Stationery also becomes outdated if your address or phone number changes, even if you don't print the pastor's name on it. I suggest you buy as much stationery as you plan to use in a reasonable time.

You can get **continuous letterhead** with holes for your computer. This paper is micro-perforated so the edge is clean when the tractor holes are torn off. If you plan to send personalized letters to visitors and others, this will be helpful to have. Plan on using continuous paper in the computer for everything so you don't have to tend the printer so closely.

Keep an inventory of all your supplies and check off what is taken from the supply cabinet so it can be reordered. This is particularly important when you are depending on volunteers.

Monitor re-ordering of supplies.

3. Sound Systems

You will probably need a sound system for worship services. If your space does not have one, and you do not have full-time use of the space, it will need to be portable. There are good portable systems available, usually sold by music stores which carry electric guitars. If you have no experience in this area, find help from someone who does. If you use all acoustic music (instruments you don't plug in), you need to know whether the instruments will need to be amplified in your space. If electric music is used, do the instruments have their own amplifiers and speakers, or will you be providing that? Do the vocalists need amplification and, if so, do they provide it? Most likely you will need a pulpit microphone and several other mikes for use by vocalists, other speakers or instruments. If your equipment can handle six inputs, you should be fine, unless you know you need more.

Aim for at least: six inputs, a mixer to control/blend them, an amplifier to carry the sound to the speakers.

All these inputs need to be controlled. That means separate volume controls for each mike and the whole unit. This requires a **mixer**, as well as an **amplifier,** speakers and wire. The mikes need stands, preferably of different styles so you have a choice. Good microphones can be expensive, so find out how many you need to start with and go from there. Will you be recording the service or playing recorded music? Get a tape deck that works with the other equipment. Find more than one person to set up and run the system on a regular basis. Several people, including the pastor, should be trained to use the system.

Radio mikes are fun and give you a lot of flexibility. You can move around without a cord, introduce visitors, etc. You are also at the mercy of your batteries and any passing vehicle with a CB radio. Weigh the pros and cons, and always have a mike with a cord ready for emergencies.

Instruments are changing these days, too. Computer control has allowed keyboard instruments to do much more than in the past. If you do not have a piano as part of your rental space, an electronic **keyboard** is probably what you will have instead. This can give both organ and piano effects as well as synthesized sounds. You may or may not need one for your keyboard player. In any event, find out whether the keyboard instrument can use your sound system or needs another system.

4. Buying or Leasing Equipment

If you buy, it is yours. If you lease, it is not. That is the basic difference. Generally, leasing is attractive to businesses because they can deduct the whole payment for income tax purposes instead of just the interest. That does not apply to a church. The other reason to lease is that you don't have the money to buy. That applies to a new church, but borrowing the money to buy will probably be cheaper than the interest in a lease. When you lease, the lease company subtracts the "salvage value" of the equipment at the end of the lease (usually there is little salvage value) from the purchase price, then figures a payment plan on the balance, plus interest. It is

"salvage value"

BORROWING EQUIPMENT

the same as buying. Few leases allow you to get out early, since the equipment has little value used. Since a church can usually get money from church-related sources rather than banks, leasing seldom makes much sense for a church.

My suggestion is that you **borrow equipment money from a church-related lender,** and give a security interest in the equipment to the lender. That way, if the church does not succeed, the lender can take the equipment for another church to use. That is the same as a commercial lender would do. Have your lawyer prepare the documents.

VI–BUDGETS

1. Income and Expenditure Budgeting

Your church budget has two parts—income and expenditures. The income budget is like a set of goals. It describes how much money is expected in different categories, mostly in offerings from the congregation. The expenditure budget is what we usually think of as a "budget" since it indicates how much will be spent for each category. Give the two types of budget separate consideration. Part of the plan should be to have more income than expenditures to create a fund for capital expenditures and cash flow leveling. You will need equipment in the future, and are probably thinking of owning a building some day, so it is appropriate to be saving toward those goals. Be sure to set savings goals for these long-range expenditures.

Some people do not feel that a church should save money. It should live on faith, spending or giving away everything it takes in. That is fine, but it can result in paying interest on borrowed money when larger items are purchased. Do whatever works for you. This is similar to the "unified budget" debate. All churches collect money to spend both internally and to give to outside causes.

If you use a unified budget, it is important that it really be unified, and that all budgeted charitable giving actually occur. Otherwise, people will give their money to other charities outside the church offering. You need to obtain reports of your congregation's giving to budgeted charities so that direct giving can be counted against the budget item. If that is done, there is no advantage in a person sending contributions directly, and the unified budget works well. A truly unified budget needs to be processed within the congregation, and people need to learn that giving is a church process, not just an individual one.

If you use an offerings system where each offering goes to a certain budget or outside item, be sure to keep your congregation informed of the amounts given. Set giving goals for those outside charities which will receive offerings, and let people know when those goals are met. Otherwise, people will send larger amounts to agencies which happen to receive favorable publicity and the church's own budget will suffer. Keep track of giving by each member and conduct an annual visit with each member. During this visit, the member's giving is noted, the church program and budget is explained, and the member has an opportunity to say what she or he thinks about the church and its budget. Keep the church's financial performance before the people and they will do their part. Taking pledges is part of this annual visit.

The budget setting process should be part of your overall setting of goals. Have goals set for a five-year period, with objectives set for the first year. The next year prepare the following year's objectives and add goals for the new fifth year. Then look at your program and budget to see whether the goals are supported by the budget. If you show your people how the goals are set and how the budget supports the goals, they will be supportive.

income and expenditures

Should a church save money?

"unified budget"

Keep the congregation informed both as a group (reports) and individually (receipts).

pledges

Set giving goals.

reporting all expenses

Many people active in churches cover certain church expenses out of their own pockets. The danger is that they will not report these expenditures, and the expenses will never get into the budget. This creates a false sense of what the program costs, and could be a surprise when the person stops paying the expense. Church planters need to discipline themselves to turn in their expenses for reimbursement. **When pastors pay church expenses out of their salary, they are cutting their pay and lulling the congregation into believing that less money is needed than is the case.** It is better to have expenses reimbursed and to then donate the same amount back to the church if a gift is intended.

2. Fiscal Year

The year doesn't necessarily end December 31. If you want your church budget year to be something else, that is fine. Since churches receive a disproportionate share of their income in December, you may want to look at a fiscal year beginning February 1. That will allow you to have a better idea of last year's income as you are establishing next year's budget.

3. Cash Flow

Determine your ''low income'' periods.

Bills are paid in cash, not pledges or good intentions. It is one thing to get pledges toward your budget, but it is another to have money in the bank ready to pay bills. **Summer is always hard on cash flow, as is the first quarter of the year.** You need to have money in the bank during those periods, or whatever your low periods turn out to be, given the facts of your local economy. You also need an alternate plan for when money is not there, particularly in the beginning.

regular financial reporting

It is tempting not to discuss giving with new people when you have a regional conference subsidy to work from. The truth is that people need to be confronted with the needs of the church from the beginning. If they are not told what the needs are, and then suddenly get panic requests for money, they will wonder about the leadership of the church. From the beginning, make it clear to your people that the church needs a certain level of income to operate, and that it can only come from those who attend. Report financial performance weekly in your worship folder, or orally if you don't yet have formal worship services. Consider a monthly written financial report. Nothing less will do. Make sure this reporting is given in a positive way.

Don't borrow to cover bad budgeting!

Plan "B" is a source for borrowing money to get through low spots. Remember that low spots are temporary; a low spot two months long is not very temporary. Summer is a problem because people are often away. Spend more energy on reminding people to continue their giving in the summer. **Consider a mailing or two during the summer, reminding people of the needs of the church and giving a cash flow report.** Enclose an envelope addressed to the church. Have an emergency plan for paying rent and pastor's salary. Borrowing outside the church or church agencies for operations is a bad idea. When you are just starting, the regional conference may well be able to help with a loan, but plan to pay it back by the end of the fiscal year. Otherwise, the loan isn't for a low spot; it's to cover bad budgeting and sloppy stewardship education. If you have clearly over-budgeted, correct it immediately. If your people are not giving to their potential, correct that.

Pastor's giving is an example to all.

tithing or ''proportionate giving''

The pastor needs to give to the church in order to preach giving. The core group also needs to be giving to their potential. There is no reason to be shy about challenging people to give to a new church. Some people prefer to speak of tithing, while others prefer the term "proportionate giving." Some suggest publishing a list of individual giving totals, without identification, so

people can see where they fit. Many people have an unrealistic idea of how much other people give. Some consultants suggest that if the pastor is in the top five of the giving list, as is usual when no list has been published, note which giving total is the pastor. A husband and wife earning above the poverty line ought to be giving a minimum of $1,000 per year, unless they are in a special situation.

4. Capital versus Expense Items

Items with a long lifetime are considered **capital items.** Items that are used or don't last long are **expense items.** You can't fund both the same way without confusing the budget. Ideally, you will have a fund for purchase of capital items, such as furniture and equipment, either from loan or subsidy, or from savings. Equipment which will need to be replaced in a reasonably short length of time should have its replacement cost calculated and budgeted into the capital fund over that period. Keep track of the individual items being saved for in the capital fund so you know how well you are doing at estimating. If you figure five years useful life for a computer, divide its cost by five and budget that amount each year into the capital fund. When the full amount is paid into the fund, you can stop paying for that item unless prices have risen enough that you should add to the fund. Be realistic about the useful life of equipment.

capital items vs. expense items

Expense items are budgeted in the usual way as ongoing expenses. If you handle your capital items as suggested, there will be little need to borrow money (at interest) for capital items, and little need for the budget to go up and down.

5. Conference and Other Charitable Giving

Your first budget should include an item for regional conference giving. It is hard to add new items to a budget as years go by. Teach your people to value your connection to the regional conference from the beginning. Perhaps you can agree with the home missions committee that gifts in the first few years will count toward repayment of loans from the regional conference. Be a full member of the regional conference by participating in its support, even if you are partly supported by it. That is just as sensible as pastors giving to the church paying their salary. Other charitable giving should be planned so that people learn to do their giving through the church. Use offerings or budget, whichever fits the situation. A unified budget is easier to start with than to introduce later, if that is your goal.

Just as individuals do, a church needs to give proportionately.

6. Loans

The basic rules for loans are: Borrow, when you must, from church or church-related sources; do not have any individual guarantee a church loan; borrow only what can be repaid from current giving by current attenders; do not borrow for operating expenses, except brief cash flow crunches which can be repaid within the fiscal year; consult conference staff and officers before borrowing from anyone, since they may have a better idea.

Churches can reasonably borrow money for major purchases such as land or buildings, but only when the item being bought has enough security to satisfy the lender. Again, do not buy property if an individual must guarantee the loan. That means the property is worth less than you are paying, or the lender doesn't want to bother with a foreclosure. The congregation must be able to make the payments on the loan out of current income, without counting on increased atten-

**loans,
cont'd**

dance or increased giving. Challenge people to increased giving before committing to build. Get pledges for the building project and have periodic special offerings for it, but use those for a down payment and later reductions of principal, not the ongoing payments. If your outreach is aimed at getting more people to pay for your mistake in overbuilding, it will not work well. People aren't that gullible.

Overbuilding does not mean building more space than your current group needs. In order to grow you need more space than you currently use. A worship space that is 80 percent full, **is** full as far as a visitor is concerned. Overbuilding means building more than your current group can pay for. For a new church, this may mean no building for quite some time, or getting a grant from the regional conference to lower the amount to be borrowed. Generally speaking, people are attracted by a combination of program and facilities, but program is most important. Cutting program to pay for facilities is self-defeating.

Churches can reasonably borrow money for larger equipment purchases such as photocopiers and computers, particularly in the beginning when there has been no opportunity to save up for these tools. The borrowing should be from church or church-related sources, and the payments should fit within your budget.

If you borrow money from individuals, particularly members of the church, be businesslike. Give them a proper promissory note, and security if that is appropriate. Have your lawyer prepare the documents. Some people may say they will forgive the note when they die. That needs to be in their will, not in the note. It is common for churches to finance major projects by borrowing from members at no interest with the whole amount due after a certain number of years. It is usually expected that many of these notes will not be repaid. Be sure that is put in the lender's will if that is their intent.

Remember, if you borrow money without any reasonable expectation of being able to repay it, that is fraud. Planning to pay it from the giving of people who have not yet begun to attend is unreasonable. A church which uses unbusinesslike practices will soon become known in the community. Pay your debts or don't make them. This also applies to the pastor's personal financial life.

**Congrega-
tional
mutual aid
helps avoid
personal
bank-
ruptcy—
which
becomes
public.**

If the pastor is in financial trouble, take care of it within the church. Don't let the public bear the burden. The same holds true to a somewhat lesser extent for all members of the church. The church should not be a scandal in the community, but should rather show the community the power of love within the community of faith.

**payroll
deductions
as loan
payments**

Loans from the church or sponsor to the pastor are fairly common. Moving expenses not paid by the church, buying a car, paying first and last months' rent on an apartment, or buying a house can all require more cash than a pastor has available. A loan is sometimes part of the initial compensation package. Be sure that the loan is not required due to the church's failure to pay expenses it should be paying. When making such a loan, be businesslike. Make a promissory note and a regular payment schedule. It may be good to have the payments made by payroll deduction. If the church intends to forgive part of the loan, that should be spelled out. If the money is to be used for a specific purpose, put that in writing as part of the agreement. To have the church council loan money for rent, and then to have the pastor buy a car, can cause conflict. If an individual loans the money, the same rules apply.

7. Model Budget

I did not comment on the budget attached to the Fresno Church Planting Proposal in Chapter II, saving that discussion for this chapter. Look at that budget as you read the following comments.

A church planting project needs a budget lasting more than one year. This one is for two years because two years of subsidy were requested. Three years is better yet, realizing that the further away a projection is, the more difficult an accurate projection becomes. We are talking about goals here. Note that the budget year starts September 1, because that is when we begin. That is a fairly realistic church fiscal year since programming tends to follow the school year. Notes explaining presuppositions are important in a budget; otherwise, the numbers mean little. We will try not to repeat the content of the budget notes here.

Every regional conference has **suggested pastor salary guidelines.** If you follow them, you won't have to spend as much energy working through the question of how much a pastor is "worth." Be sure to include in the budget **pension plan contributions** for the pastor. Plan to use the regional conference pension plan. It will be more sensitive to the needs of your pastor than an unrelated group would be. If you cannot afford to pay a full-time salary, hire the pastor part-time rather than having a low full-time salary. It is easier to increase the pastor's time than to give a pay raise. That will also eliminate the situation where the next pastor has an artificially low salary. If a pastor is working part-time, be sure to have a clear understanding of what time commitment is expected, and how the other time will be spent.

The telemarketing item covers mainly office supplies and telephone installation. You will need to find out about local telephone installation costs and make an estimate on supplies. Rent is always a difficult item to budget before a place is actually found. Some research will put you in the right price range. Rent for worship equipment in this case means chairs, since we are looking at places that don't have them. If the place we get does not have them, but could store them, we would buy instead of rent. Your office supplies item will be larger. Start-up expenses are low in this budget because we have a lot of office equipment.

The regional conference travel item included in this budget is for specific regional conference sessions. Your budget should also reflect your particular situation. This item is often included in a pastor's salary, since it is for the pastor, but that gives a false picture of what the pastor is paid. The same applies to the automobile allowance, which is reimbursement for use of the pastor's car. That money goes to the pastor, but is not "pay." Agree how the car allowance will be paid. Is it based on actual miles or is it a flat fee? If it is based on actual mileage, a monthly report and reimbursement is appropriate, perhaps paid in advance. If it is a flat fee, it should be paid monthly. Decide how mileage in excess of the budget will be handled. The item for equipment service includes the copier and computer.

Not shown in the budget is a $7,000 loan for capital expenditures from Pacific District Conference. That will cover equipment such as copier and computer. It will be loaned as needed, since we won't buy everything at once and may get better deals on some things. The church's giving to regional conference will count as payments on the loan.

Income budgeting is simple, but reflects much thought on what is reasonable to expect in offerings and gifts from friends. There is no fat in the budget; in fact, it is too lean in spots, having no item for memberships, media or advertising. A typical church planting would need less for rent than a church using telemarketing since no large worship space is needed for a longer period of time. The income budget for local giving is relatively ambitious in this budget.

This is not a unified budget. There is no charitable giving in it. We plan to discuss this with our core group and make a decision on the best way for our particular situation to handle its giving.

8. Bookkeeping Systems

There are many bookkeeping systems out there, both manual and computer-based. If you buy a church software package for your computer, it will have a bookkeeping package in it. Earlier we discussed the pros and cons of computer bookkeeping. Whatever system you use, discuss it with your accountant and have the accountant start you on the right foot. You want a system that is easy enough to use that it will be kept up-to-date. Let your treasurer help decide what will be best. If the treasurer uses a home computer, make sure it is compatible with the church computer, so that when treasurers change, you aren't left with an incompatible system. Check into having your accountant do bookkeeping from the treasurer's income and check writing records. It may be an inexpensive way to save volunteer labor.

Remember that there will be the usual income and expenditure items to keep track of, and also individual giving and giving to charitable causes. If you create the capital expenditures fund, those items will need to be tracked. All this needs regular reports or it is useless. Be sure the system lends itself to regular reporting. A manual system can still be assisted by computer word processing. A standard report form can be kept in the church computer so that only the numbers need to be typed in to have a good report that leaves nothing out. Try to include giving graphs in your reports so people get a sense of the ebb and flow of cash.

Regular maintenance is the key.

No system will be any good if it is not maintained regularly. Make sure your treasurer keeps the records current. Old financial information doesn't help much. The pastor should not know how much individuals give, but should be informed when there has been a sudden change in a member's giving pattern. That will often signal a pastoral care need. The same goes for attendance.

VII—CLOSING THOUGHTS

There is more to church planting than technical and legal details. While we have discussed many things in this book, they are only a small slice of the life of the church. Technical details can cause problems if they aren't handled properly. If they are processed in timely fashion, they will not occupy much of a church planter's time. It is my hope, and the hope of the sponsors of this book, that by giving you the kinds of details we have provided here, you will be able to spend less time on administration and more on ministry. May all our efforts be to the glory of God.

Appendix A

FLOWCHART FOR ORGANIZATION/INCORPORATION

1. Obtain attorney, accountant and other consultants.

2. Obtain state/province information regarding organization/incorporation and taxation, including employer's tax information.

3. Choose names of church and incorporators.

4. Prepare and file Articles of Incorporation (where permitted).

5. Obtain Employer's Tax Identification Number (U.S.).

6. Hold organizational meeting of first board of directors.
   a. Adopt bylaws/constitution
   b. Select officers
   c. Adopt banking resolutions
   d. Adopt fiscal year
   e. Transfer assets of church in organization to corporation
   f. Hire pastor (see following appendix for contract form)

7. Obtain tax exemptions—federal, state, local—including property tax and sales tax.

8. Set up books of account and bank accounts.

9. Prepare W-4 forms (U.S.).

10. Obtain bulk mailing permit (U.S.).

Appendix B

ARTICLES OF INCORPORATION

The required contents of Articles of Incorporation vary from state to state and province to province, although the variation is small. What follows are the sample Articles for a church provided by the California Secretary of State, with comments or suggested material in brackets.

Articles of Incorporation of Any Church

Notes

(This will vary in different jurisdictions.)

I
The name of this corporation is (Any Church).

II
A. This corporation is a religious corporation and is not organized for the private gain of any person. It is organized under the Nonprofit Religious Corporation Law exclusively for religious purposes.

(This is the place where doctrinal material would be inserted. It is my suggestion that you not put doctrinal material in the Articles, including a statement of affiliation with a conference/district since names of conferences/districts and particular wording of doctrinal points changes, and would require amendment of the Articles.)

B. The specific purpose of this corporation is to operate a church.

(The agent for service of process is the person who receives the papers when you are sued. Be sure you name a knowledgeable person for this task. If papers are ever served on the agent, they must take them immediately to a lawyer for interpretation. There are strict time limits for responding.)

III
The name and address in the state of California of this corporation's initial agent for service of process is (name and address).

(This section is straight from the Internal Revenue Code, and applies only to U.S. congregations. This must be in your Articles for you to be tax exempt, in exactly the required words. Your lawyer will tell you if there are any recent changes in the required wording. With this section in the Articles, a member of the congregation could use the courts to stop any activity by the board or officers in violation of this section. You will be glad to know that the usual preaching and teaching function of the church does not violate this section. It is when the church goes public with its political opinions that it is in violation. A separate

IV
A. This corporation is organized and operated exclusively for religious purposes within the meaning of Section 501(c)(3) of the Internal Revenue Code.

B. No substantial part of the activities of this corporation shall consist of carrying on propaganda, or otherwise intending to influence legislation, and the corporation shall not participate or intervene in any political campaign (including the publishing or distribution of statements) on behalf of any candidate for public office.

66

V

The property of this corporation is irrevocably dedicated to religious purposes and no part of the net income or assets of this corporation shall ever inure to the benefit of any director, officer or member thereof, or to the benefit of any private person. Upon the dissolution of the corporation, its assets remaining after payment, or provision for payment, of all debts and liabilities of this corporation shall be distributed to a nonprofit fund, foundation or corporation which is organized and operated exclusively for religious purposes and which has established its tax exempt status under Section 501(c)(3) of the Internal Revenue Code.

Date:

(Signature of incorporator)
(Typed name of incorporator)

I hereby declare that I am (we are) the person(s) who executed the foregoing Articles of Incorporation, which execution is my (our) act and deed.

(Signature of incorporator)

organization which is not tax exempt would need to be formed to carry on lobbying activities. Most political action organizations have two corporations, one for the usual public education activities, which is tax exempt, and the other for activities aimed at influencing legislation or elections, which is not tax exempt. Individual members can do as they please. It is only when official action of the church steps over the line that there is a problem.)

(The General Conference Mennonite Church (or other appropriate conference), its successors or assigns, is hereby designated as the nonprofit corporation to receive such assets.)

(This is another paragraph straight from the Internal Revenue Code. It is the Irrevocable Dedication Clause mentioned in Chapter III, and applies only to U.S. congregations. This paragraph must be included in the Articles for you to be tax exempt. Do not change one jot or tittle of the required wording, and check with a lawyer for any recent changes in the required wording. The last sentence is one you can change as is appropriate for your situation.)

(I show the signature block because, at least in California, no variation from the approved form is acceptable. I have tried various tiny changes over the years, and they have been rejected. You really do have to sign it and then sign it saying you signed it. When I tried to use one signature, it was rejected. This shows how important it is to have a lawyer advise you on the requirements of your state or province. Even lawyers make mistakes. Many jurisdictions use a printed form for Articles. You must use that form where one is provided.)

Appendix C

PASTOR CONTRACT

Most congregations have some sort of written document explaining the agreement they have with their pastor. Commonly this is called a Memorandum of Understanding. It is usual for this memorandum to describe pay and benefits, but not to contain a job description. What follows is based on the Sample Memos of Understanding distributed by the Western District Conference of the General Conference Mennonite Church, and the Conference of Mennonites in Canada. This sample presumes that a document will be typed, and it contains various notes which are not to be part of the final document. Whatever the document is called, it becomes a legally binding contract when signed, and your lawyer should review it.

Notes

Looking at the sample memo, it calls for a fixed term. In usual practice a **fixed term** is not very fixed, since a pastor is free to resign at any time. It does give a certain stability, and makes it likely that even an unhappy congregation will wait until the contract runs its course. Regular reviews are suggested, and a plan for conducting regular reviews should be attached.

The salary and housing paragraphs allow for a **housing allowance** to be named. This is not taxable income, so it is to the pastor's advantage to have it set as high as possible under current rules. Check out current rules with an accountant or your denominational business office. The understanding of when certain types of maintenance will be done should be listed. Items such as interior painting should definitely be discussed at contract time.

Pension plans are important, particularly for pastors who live in a parsonage and will have to buy a house upon retirement. The Mennonite Church uses Mennonite Retirement Trust and the General Conference Mennonite Church uses Presbyterian Ministers' Fund. In Canada, the Canada Pension is an important difference. Church planters should have pension contributions like any other pastor.

Health insurance is important, and in the U.S., Mennonite pastors generally use Mennonite Mutual Aid. Having a sick day policy becomes important when there is an extended illness. Disability insurance can also be an important part of the sick leave policy. Consider providing disability insurance in a long-term disability situation while the con-

Sample Memo of Understanding
Between Pastor and Any Church

1. Term. The pastor's term will be (_____) years, beginning (date) and ending (date). There will be an annual review of the relationship between the pastor and church conducted by the (group).

2. Salary. The church will pay the pastor a cash salary of ($ amount) per year in twice monthly installments of ($ amount).

3. Housing. ($ amount) of the pastor's salary shall be designated as a housing allowance. OR, the Church shall provide the Pastor and family with a parsonage furnished with (list). The church is responsible for all repairs and maintenance of the parsonage, and will repaint the interior with colors acceptable to the pastor prior to the pastor's arrival. The interior will be repainted within five years, unless otherwise agreed. The church will pay for utilities for the parsonage except for personal long distance phone calls. OR, a utilities allowance of ($ amount) per month will be paid to the pastor, to be reviewed annually.

4. Pension. (U.S.) The church will pay into the pastor's pension plan with (Name) an annual amount equal to ten percent of the pastor's cash salary.
(Canada) The church will pay five percent of the cash salary into the regional conference (or other) pension plan and the Canada Pension Plan, with the pastor contributing an additional five percent. The church and pastor participate in the Canadian Unemployment Insurance Plan according to the regulations of the Unemployment Insurance Division.

5. Health insurance. (U.S.) The church will pay the quarterly assessment to enroll the pastor and family in the current Mennonite Mutual Aid, Inc. health insurance program with a $500 deductible.
(Canada) The church will pay the health or hospitalization premium where one is charged by the province.

6. Holidays and sick days. The pastor shall have all national legal holidays. Where such holidays fall on church celebration

days, a compensatory day at a more convenient time will be taken. The pastor shall have one day per month sick leave, cumulative to 12 days. Unused sick days will be paid for, in cash, upon termination at the rate of 1/365 of the then current annual cash salary per day accumulated.

7. Disability insurance. The church shall provide a policy of disability insurance for the pastor as described in the attached declarations page. (Various conferences/districts sponsor disability plans.)

8. Continuing education. The church shall provide the pastor with ($ amount) per year for books, subscriptions, dues to professional organizations and continuing education events. After seven years of service, the pastor shall have three months educational leave. By virtue of service in a prior congregation, (amount) years shall be credited toward this service.

9. Conference activities. Registration fees and travel expenses for attendance by the pastor at (name) regional conference sessions will be paid by the church, and no vacation time will be deducted for such attendance and necessary travel.

10. Automobile. The church will pay (amount) per mile for use of the pastor's personal automobile on church business. Mileage for any trip shall not exceed the standard airfare for such trip.

11. Office expenses. The church will provide all reasonable office equipment and supplies, including postage and telephone for use on church business. The pastor may make reasonable personal use of such equipment and supplies.

12. Vacation. The church grants the pastor (amount) weeks per year vacation. A normal work week shall equal 14 units (morning, afternoon or evening). The church shall pay for pulpit supply during absences of the pastor as set out in this Memo. The pastor will inform the appropriate church officers of planned absences as far in advance as possible.

13. Reporting. The pastor will report directly to (name) and to such other groups as may be appropriate.

14. Review. The terms of this Memo will be reviewed annually prior to developing and approving the church budget.

Signatures

gregation covers the first three to six months. Such insurance is very inexpensive. This is different in Canada where most health care is covered by government health plans.

Continuing education is particularly important for church planters since the field is growing so rapidly. Research and the experience of others can make a difference. All pastors need some continuing education to stay sharp. The same goes for regional conference travel. It is important for a church planter to be with other church planters.

Automobile allowance on a mileage basis is reasonable. In the U.S. it is becoming more complicated to deduct business mileage. Check current rules. In Canada, at this writing, the automobile allowance is not reportable income for tax purposes.

Vacation should be carefully spelled out. Does conference and continuing education come out of vacation? Who decides? Sabbaticals should be considered. The problem is that the average pastoral tenure is less than the seven years normally considered appropriate before a sabbatical is granted. If all congregations gave a sabbatical after a pastor had been in ministry seven years, it would be no problem. Since they don't, consider granting a smaller sabbatical after four or five years, and another several years later. That's a long time away for a church planting project, but it will come before you know it. This sample suggests giving credit toward the sabbatical for prior service.

Spend much energy in the beginning deciding how the pastor/congregation partnership will be reviewed. How will the pastor know how the congregation views continued tenure? Make plans while everyone is smiling. Your regional conference minister is the one to help you with this. As the congregation makes the transition to full self-government, establish a pastor relations committee to be the lightning rod for both pastor and congregation. There need be no nasty surprises for anyone if everyone pays attention.

Appendix D

WORKSHEET FOR A CHURCH PLANTING PROPOSAL
(See Chapter II for further information)

PRELIMINARY MISSION STATEMENT AND PHILOSOPHY OF MINISTRY
For a Church to Be Planted in Any Town

Why is this church to be planted?
Be specific. What is it that drives you to plant this church? What is your call? What is the dream?

What kind of church is to be planted?
Once again, be specific. Tell how this church will be the same or different. What flavor? What distinctives? In what areas will this congregation focus its energies? Describe worship style, group life, pastoral care strategy. How large is the group you hope to gather? Are you generic evangelical, Anabaptist, what? Then say what that means. How do you envision outreach ministries being carried out?

Where is this church to be planted?
This is where you incorporate the results of your demographic study to explain why you picked the location. If you haven't done the demographic study, do that before writing the proposal.

What group of persons will this church hope to attract?
The demographic study comes into play here again. Are the people you are targeting living in the area you are targeting? Why do you feel called to this group of people? Are you suited by ethnicity, regional background, language, educational level and/or personality to minister to them?

Who will sponsor this church?
Name one or more congregations and the regional conference planning to be involved, or to which you are directing this proposal. Describe why the congregation(s) is right for the job, and how this has been processed with them. Which is the primary sponsor to have direct oversight? What denominational affiliation(s) is planned.

How will this church be planted?
Be specific. How do you plan to do it? Lay out the method and timetable with all goals as appropriate.

When will this church be planted?
The timetable in graphic form. When do you start?

What sort of pastoral leadership will this church have?
Describe the person(s) you either have or will seek. What kind of people are they? What are their gifts? How will they work together with other leaders? What are their strengths and weaknesses? How do you see them capitalizing on the strengths and working with the weaknesses?

How will oversight be provided?
To whom will you be accountable? If you are using the support group plan outlined in this book, describe the group you have formed or plan to form. If you want the organization to which you are presenting this proposal to provide people for the support group or to provide an overseer, say so.

What will make this church a Mennonite church (or other denomination)?
What will the specific distinctives be?

What worship style will predominate?
Since this is the single most important issue next to the personality of the pastor, think it out carefully. Who are you as a worshiping church? We aren't accustomed to describing our worship styles, but you should here. How does this worship style fit your target group?

What will be the strategy of evangelism?
Will it be to have members of childbearing age, or something more assertive? Spell out in some detail how you plan to grow and remain viable.

The budget portion of the proposal is separate, but needs to be complete. See Chapter II for a sample budget and discussion.

Signatures and dates

Appendix E

SAMPLE FORMS

Forms attached include:

Monthly Project Report, for use by church planter to report to sponsor and/or regional conference committee

Mennonite Board of Missions Funding Request Procedures

MBM Church Development Funding Request Packet

MBM Congregational Progress Report

MONTHLY REPORT

Congregation: _____ Month ending: _____

1. Activities:

    Positive response to telecomputer   _____

    Visits to new persons   _____

    Study/preparation hours   _____

    Community contacts
    (e.g. ecumenical gatherings, school, etc.)   _____

    Teaching times with congregational
    participants   _____

List some highlights from last months contacts with the unchurched:

List some highlights of last months assimilation of new persons (e.g.
involving, building friendship between people, etc.):

2. Attendance: Worship   _____

                       Small groups - How many? _____   Average attendance ____

                       Other gatherings   _____

3. Reflection on last month: What worked well? What problems occurred?

4. Vision for next month - What are some of your goals for next month?

5. Family & personal: What are you doing for . . .
    . . . fun and relaxation?

    . . . personal growth?

    . . . family enrichment?

6. Prayer requests:

Mennonite Board of Missions
FUNDING REQUEST PROCEDURES

To request funding from MBM, a Funding Request form must be completed.
This form outlines the total financial package for the project for
which funds are being sought.

The conference mission leader should complete this form in cooperation
with a congregational leader. Also include the leadership commission
chairman of the conference when pastoral support is involved.

Normally the funding received from MBM will follow the 5-year phaseout
schedule as outlined in the Funding Principles paper. Using that
phaseout schedule as a guide, compute the dollar amounts for each of
the years funding is anticipated. Be sure to include the beginning
date of the project, as the deduction in funding will happen on the
anniversary month of the project; e.g., if the project began September
1, 1985, the second-year amount of funding will begin September 1,
1986.

Each project which is receiving partnership grants from MBM will need
to complete a Congregational Progress Report. The Progress Report is
to be completed by the pastor and returned to the conference office.
The conference office will submit the white copy of the Progress
Reports with their annual funding requests to MBM.

IMPORTANT:

1. Complete the forms, making sure all four copies are legible.

2. Answer each question as thoroughly as possible, leaving no blanks.

3. Have the proper signatures affixed to the funding request.

4. When the forms are fully completed, keep the goldenrod copy for
    your records and return the other 3 copies to Evangelism and Church
    Development, Mennonite Board of Missions, Box 370, Elkhart,
    Indiana 46515.

5. Send a copy of the congregation's budget and program goals/
    objectives to MBM with the funding request forms.

The funding requests submitted to MBM will be presented to the MBM
Board of Directors for budget allocation. Following that, the approved
requests will be signed by MBM, and copies of the request forms will be
sent to the mission board/commission leader for distribution to the
appropriate persons.

4-8-86
MM

74

Mennonite
Board of Missions
Box 370 • Elkhart IN 46515-0370

CHURCH DEVELOPMENT FUNDING REQUEST

Church _____

Address_____

_____

Pastor _____

Address_____

_____ Phone ( )_____

Supervisor/overseer of project _____

Number of persons in group _____

Check as many as appropriate:

( ) Urban
( ) Suburban
( ) Small Town
( ) Rural

( ) Low Income
( ) Middle Income
( ) Upper Income

( ) Anglo
( ) Asian (language _____)
( ) Black
( ) Hispanic
( ) Native American _____
( ) Other_____

Program goals/projections: (list on a separate sheet of paper and attach)

CHURCH PROGRAM BUDGET FOR 19 ____

EXPENSES

Pastor's Salary	$_____
Housing	_____
Hospitalization	_____
Retirement	_____
Other	_____ $_____
Supplies	_____
Utilities	_____
Other: _____	_____
Other: _____	_____
TOTAL	$_____

INCOME

Congregation	$_____
Conference	$_____
Other	$_____
MBM	$_____
TOTAL	$_____

_____
(Congregational Leader signature)

_____
(Conference signature)

_____
(Mennonite Board of Missions signature)

_____
Date

PHASE OUT SCHEDULE

Beginning date of project _____

	Conf.	MBM
Year 1	$_____	$_____
Year 2	$_____	$_____
Year 3	$_____	$_____
Year 4	$_____	$_____
Year 5	$_____	$_____

75

CONGREGATIONAL PROGRESS REPORT
(to be completed by the pastor)

Congregational Program
1. What types of programs/activities does your congregation have?

		Average attendance
_____	Sunday worship services	_____
_____	Sunday School	_____
_____	Sunday evening services	_____
_____	Bible study/prayer meeting groups	_____
_____	Youth activities	_____
_____	Social events	_____
_____	Business meetings	_____
_____	_____	_____
_____	_____	_____
_____	_____	_____

Membership
2. What is your congregation's membership? _____

3. During the past year, indicate number of member gains and losses:

	Gains		Losses
_____	Biological--from your church family	_____	Transfer - Move out of community
_____	Transfer--from another congregation	_____	Transfer - To other local church
_____	Conversion--from non-church background	_____	Dropout - No longer attending anywhere
_____	Recommitment--from inactive status	_____	Deaths

Leadership Training
4. Have you provided any leadership training for the lay leaders in your congregation?
Yes _____ No _____. If yes, please describe and list material used.

Outreach
5. How are you getting acquainted with your community?

6. How many new contacts did you make in your community during the past year? _____

7. What methods are you using to increase Sunday attendance?

8. How much increase do you anticipate in Sunday attendance? _____

9. How do you plan to expand your weekly activities?

<u>Budget</u> Please enclose a copy of your congregation's current expense and income statement (budget).

10. Did your congregation meet last year's budget? Yes _____ No _____

11. How many family units are regularly involved in the church life? _____

12. What was the total contribution to the church by the involved family units during the past year? $_____

13. Approximately how many family units gave 10 percent or more to the church? _____

<u>Goals</u>
14. What are the current goals of your congregation? (Please attach)

<u>Your Experience</u>
15. How is it going for you? How do you personally feel about the past year?

16. Are you receiving adequate supervision/mentoring/resourcing from the conference to which you relate?

17. In what areas would you appreciate additional assistance?

Thank you for your assistance.

Date _____   Signed _____

                                     Congregation _____

                                     Address _____

Form prepared by Mennonite Board of Missions, Box 370, Elkhart, Indiana 46515.

Page 2 of 2

Appendix F

CHURCH ADMINISTRATION COMPUTER SOFTWARE

Computer retail stores are able to locate church administration software when they are given the name of the software company which created it or the name of the software package. They do not have lists of software by type. A list of church administration software is available from:

> Churchwide EDP
> Presbyterian Church (U.S.A.)
> 475 Riverside Dr. Room 1908
> New York, NY 10115
> (212) 870-3403

This office is in the process of moving as this book is being written, so check with a nearby Presbyterian church for the new address. Your denominational office may also be able to provide you with information regarding software packages in use within your denomination. What follows is a list of companies from the Presbyterian list which have written integrated church administration software packages which appear to be of possible use to church planters. I have no personal experience with any of these packages, nor do I know anyone who has used them. This field is quite new. You may wish to contact several of the larger churches in your area to find out what they are using.

International MicroSystems
6445 Metcalf
Shawnee Mission, KS 66202

Ecclesiastical Management Assoc
7086 Carlisle Pike
Carlisle, PA 17013

E Z Systems, Inc
214 Mockingbird Rd.
Nashville, TN 37205

Data Services, Inc.
233 Office Plaza, Suite 2
Tallahassee, FL 32301

Church Growth Data Services
150 S. Los Robles Ave., #600
Pasadena, CA 91101

Christian Computer/Based
  Communications
44 Delma Dr.
Toronto, ON M8W 4N6
Canada

Hardman-Myers Associates
3504 Lowlen Ct.
Ellicott City, MD 21043

ERB Software
PO Box 58713
Houston, TX 77258

Disciple Data, Inc.
PO Box 7058
Indianapolis, IN 46207

Cybertronics, Inc.
990 Payne Ave.
St. Paul, MN 55101

Church-Related Computer
  Programming
305 SE Terrace
Roseburg, OR 97470

The largest selling package was developed for Lutheran churches, and is available through the following stores:

Augsburg Publishing House
Box 1209
Minneapolis, MN 55440

Concordia Publishing House
3558 S. Jefferson St.
St. Louis, MO 63118

Fortress Church Supply Stores
2900 Queen Ln
Philadelphia, PA 19129

All of these packages sell for several hundred to several thousand dollars. The list of suppliers available from Presbyterian EDP has over 100 names.

BIBLIOGRAPHY

Alphabetical list. * Denotes priority reading. A church beginning to look at the subject may want to purchase all of these for its library.

Chaney, Charles L. *Church Planting at the End of the Twentieth Century.* Wheaton, Ill.: Tyndale House Publishers, Inc., 1986. Looks particularly at the possibilities for church planting in transitional communities. Many charts and figures. Gives much data to support homogeneous unit principal, and shows that the Apostle Paul was fighting for homogeneous unit principal at the Jerusalem conference.

Conn, Harvie M. *A Clarified Vision for Urban Mission*. Grand Rapids, Mich.: Zondervan Publishing House, 1987. I had trouble reading this book because I kept jumping up to read things from it to my wife. All the statistics you ever need to preach on urban evangelism.

Hoge, Dean R. and Roozen, David A., editors. *Understanding Church Growth and Decline 1950-1978.* New York, N.Y.: The Pilgrim Press, 1979. Everything you ever wanted to know about the subject, and then some. During this period, churches had unprecedented growth, followed by the first decline in Christian history. The mainline denominations lost 50 percent of their members. Important reading for anyone wanting to help the church grow.

McGavran, Donald A. *Understanding Church Growth* (rev. ed.). Grand Rapids, Mich.: William B. Eerdmans Publishing Co., 1980. This book began the modern church growth movement. Has more of an overseas perspective, but that is valuable as we begin to think of North American church planting as the mission work it is.

Nikkel, James. *Antioch Blueprints.* Winnipeg, Man.: Board of Evangelism, Canadian Conference of Mennonite Brethren Churches, 1987. A notebook covering the entire spectrum from inception of a church planting project through program development. A support manual of the Centennial Antioch Plan of the CCMBC. Covers the topic, but is thin in spots, particularly the areas covered by *A Technical Manual for Church Planters*. Offers a concise compilation of church growth wisdom.

*Peace, Richard. *Small Group Evangelism.* Downers Grove, Ill.: InterVarsity Press, 1985. Excellent guide to forming and running small groups for evangelistic purposes. If you have non-Christian friends, how do you share the gospel with them? This book tells how. Designed to be studied by a group committed to small group evangelism, and leads the group through a training process. Also valuable for individual reading. Has a succinct presentation of the gospel.

Redford, Jack. **Planting New Churches.** Nashville, Tenn.: Broadman Press, 1978. A Southern Baptist book which needs much adaptation for Mennonites. Good if you want to follow their model, which is quite specific. A helpful book for churches interested in church planting by the swarm method.

Shenk, Wilbert R., editor. **Exploring Church Growth.** Grand Rapids, Mich.: William B. Eerdmans Publishing Co., 1983. Focuses on overseas. One of the few books on the subject from a Mennonite perspective.

*Stoll, Dale. **Church Planting: From Seed to Harvest.** Mennonite Board of Missions, Elkhart, Ind., and General Conference Mennonite Church, Newton, Kan., 1986. A popularly written beginners' guide to the subject. *READ THIS BOOK FIRST.*

*Tillapaugh, Frank R. **Unleashing the Church.** Ventura, Calif.: Regal Books, 1982. This is a dangerous book if you are comfortable in your church life and don't want anything to change. A series of three videos with Frank giving the gist of the book in a seminar setting is available and excellent for group use.

Towns, Elmer. **Getting a Church Started**. Lynchburg, Va.: Church Growth Institute, 1985. An excellent step-by-step guide to the independent Baptist style of church planting. Lots of good material, but needs adaptation for Mennonites and others not oriented toward independent churches.

*Wagner, C. Peter. **Leading Your Church to Growth**. Ventura, Calif.: Regal Books, 1984. All about leadership. Church planters need to be different from pastors of established churches. This book explains how. Mennonites are in transition on the issue of leadership style. The servant/leader model we have been trying to follow for the last 15-20 years does not result in church growth or successful church planting. Wagner, one of the fathers of the church growth movement, shows how we may want to be for the next period in history.

Wimber, John. **Power Evangelism.** San Francisco, Calif.: Harper & Row, 1986. Charismatic evangelism for those who would like to know how it is different. Very readable. How can this style inform yours? Wimber's Vineyard Ministries offers other books and seminars on church planting, using evangelistic small groups which are quite adaptable to groups not using a charismatic worship style.

*Zunkel, C. Wayne. **Church Growth Under Fire.** Scottdale, Pa.: Herald Press, 1987. A fun book, written from the standpoint of responding to criticism. A must for anyone interested in the area of church growth. This Church of the Brethren author speaks a language Mennonites can understand.